ROUTLEDGE LIBRARY EDITIONS: JAPAN

A HISTORY OF JAPAN

A HISTORY OF JAPAN

HISHO SAITO

Translated by
ELIZABETH LEE

Volume 44

LONDON AND NEW YORK

First published in 1912

This edition first published in 2011
by Routledge
2 Park Square, Milton Park, Abingdon, Oxon, OX14 4RN

Simultaneously published in the USA and Canada
by Routledge
711 Third Avenue, New York, NY 10017

Routledge is an imprint of the Taylor & Francis Group, an informa business

© 1912 Kegan Paul, Trench, Trübner & Co., Ltd

First issued in paperback 2013

All rights reserved. No part of this book may be reprinted or reproduced or utilised in any form or by any electronic, mechanical, or other means, now known or hereafter invented, including photocopying and recording, or in any information storage or retrieval system, without permission in writing from the publishers.

British Library Cataloguing in Publication Data
A catalogue record for this book is available from the British Library

ISBN 13: 978-0-415-58538-5 (hbk)

ISBN 13: 978-0-203-84507-3 (pbk)

Publisher's Note
The publisher has gone to great lengths to ensure the quality of this reprint but points out that some imperfections in the original copies may be apparent.

Disclaimer
The publisher has made every effort to trace copyright holders and would welcome correspondence from those they have been unable to trace.

A
HISTORY OF JAPAN

BY
HISHO SAITO

TRANSLATED BY
ELIZABETH LEE

LONDON
KEGAN PAUL, TRENCH, TRÜBNER & Co., Ltd
Broadway House, Carter Lane, E.C.
1912

CONTENTS

PAGE

INTRODUCTION.

THE EARLIEST INHABITANTS OF JAPAN. ORIGIN OF THE JAPANESE. THE OLDEST HISTORICAL SOURCES ... 1

FIRST PERIOD.

FROM THE BEGINNING OF THE EMPIRE TO THE FALL OF THE SOGA FAMILY ... 5

PART I.

FROM THE BEGINNING OF THE EMPIRE TO THE SUBJECTION OF KOREA ... 5

CHAPTER I.—Foundation of the Japanese Empire. The first Emperor ... 7

CHAPTER II.—Relations with Korea. Struggles with the native races. State of civilization ... 11

CHAPTER III.—The subjection of Korea ... 16

PART II.

FROM THE INTRODUCTION OF CHINESE CULTURE TO THE FALL OF THE SOGA FAMILY ... 19

CHAPTER IV.—The introduction of Chinese culture into Japan. Economic progress of the nation ... 21

CHAPTER V.—The rebellion of Korea ... 24

CHAPTER VI.—The beginnings of Buddhism in Japan 26
CHAPTER VII.—The regency of the Crown Prince Shokotu. Direct Intercourse with China. Further Introduction of Chinese culture and of Buddhism 30
CHAPTER VIII.—The fall of the Soga Family . 33

SECOND PERIOD.

FROM THE TAIKA REFORMS TO THE FALL OF THE TAIRA FAMILY 37

PART I.

FROM THE TAIKA REFORMS TO THE FOUNDATION OF THE CAPITAL, KIOTO 37

CHAPTER I.—The Taika reforms 39
CHAPTER II.—The Ainu insurrection. End of Japanese rule in Korea. Continuation of reform 41
CHAPTER III.—Reforms of the first Taihō year . 44
CHAPTER IV.—The Seven Courts of Nara. Buddhism, Art and Learning 47
CHAPTER V.—Foundation of the town of Kioto. The great period of learning and further progress of Buddhism 51

PART II.

THE AGE OF THE FUJIWARA 55

CHAPTER VI.—The increasing power of the Fujiwara 57
CHAPTER VII.—Futile attempts to destroy the power of the Fujiwara. Art and learning of the period 59

CONTENTS

CHAPTER VIII.—The beginnings of the feudal system 61
CHAPTER IX.—The Fujiwara family as guardians of the state. Japanese influence on Chinese civilization 64

PART III.

THE TAIRA AND MINAMOTO 69

CHAPTER X.—Abolition of government by guardians of the Fujiwara Family, and Emperors who had abdicated. Growing power of the Taira and Minamoto 71
CHAPTER XI.—Strife in the Imperial Family. Supremacy of the Taira and Minamoto . . 74
CHAPTER XII.—Hostility between the Taira and Minamoto 76
CHAPTER XIII.—Supremacy and fall of the Taira . 78

THIRD PERIOD.

FROM THE FOUNDATION OF THE KAMAKURA SHOGUNATE TO THE END OF THE TOKUGAWA SHOGUNATE (FEUDAL PERIOD) 83

PART I.

THE KAMAKURA SHOGUNATE 83

CHAPTER I.—Foundation of the Kamakura Shogunate by the Minamoto family. Their supremacy and their fall through the Hojo family . . 85
CHAPTER II.—Establishment of the supremacy of the Hojo Family. *Fainéant* Shoguns and Skikken 89
CHAPTER III.—Repulse of Mongolian attempts at invasion 91

CHAPTER IV.—Art, learning and religion at the time of the Kamakura Shōgunate . . . 93
CHAPTER V.—Division of the Imperial line. Abolition of the Shōgunate 96

PART II.

RESTORATION, DIVISION AND RECONCILIATION OF THE IMPERIAL DYNASTY 99

CHAPTER VI.—Reign and fall of Go-Daigo-Tennō 101
CHAPTER VII.—Dynasties of the North and South 104

PART III.

THE MUROMACHI OR ASHIKAGA SHOGUNATE . . 107

CHAPTER VIII.—The Muromachi Shōgunate . 109
CHAPTER IX.—The disorders of the Onin years and the struggle for the supremacy of Kamakura 112
CHAPTER X.—The age of Higashiyama. Art, literature and learning 116
CHAPTER XI.—The Heroic Age, (1478-1573) . 118
CHAPTER XII.—Relations with foreign lands . 124

PART IV.

THE ODA AND TOYOTOMI FAMILIES (1573-1598) . . 127

CHAPTER XIII.—Oda Nobunaga 129
CHAPTER XIV.—The conquest and union of the whole Empire by Toyotomi-Hideyoshi . . 133
CHAPTER XV.—Toyotomi-Hideyoshi's foreign enterprises 137
CHAPTER XVI.—The decisive battle between the Toyotomi and Tokugawa families. Victory of the Tokugawa family 140

CONTENTS ix.

PART V.

THE TOKUGAWA SHOGUNATE 143

CHAPTER XVII.—Establishment of the Tokugawa Shogunate 145
CHAPTER XVIII.—Bushidō 150
CHAPTER XIX.—Relations with foreign countries 156
CHAPTER XX.—Spread and suppression of Christianity 161
CHAPTER XXI.—The Reigns of Ieyasu's Successors. Flourishing state of art and learning. Beginning of economic progress 165
CHAPTER XXII.—The most flourishing period of the Tokugawa Shōgunate 169
CHAPTER XXIII.—End of the great period of prosperity of the Tokugawa Shōgunate . . 172
CHAPTER XXIV.—The awakening of a public opinion. Intellectual tendencies towards the revival of the Imperial power and the opening of the country to Europeans 174
CHAPTER XXV.—Conclusion of the first commercial treaty 178
CHAPTER XXVI.—Fall of the Shōgunate. Restoration of the Imperial power 184

FOURTH PERIOD.

MEIJI. 191

CHAPTER I.—Beginning of the Meiji age . . 193
CHAPTER II.—Reaction against the new system of government 207
CHAPTER III.—Introduction of constitutional government 213

CONTENTS

	PAGE
CHAPTER IV.—Relations of Japan with Russia and with Korea	218
CHAPTER V.—The Chino-Japanese war . .	222
CHAPTER VI.—The revision of the commercial treaties	230
CHAPTER VII.—The Chinese troubles . . .	232
CHAPTER VIII.—The Russo-Japanese War .	236

AINU FAMILY

A History of Japan

INTRODUCTION.

THE EARLIEST INHABITANTS OF JAPAN. ORIGIN OF THE JAPANESE. THE OLDEST HISTORICAL SOURCES.

THE Japanese are not indigenous to their land. They first came to their present home at the end of the bronze or the beginning of the iron age.

Philological research decisively proves that the people who dwelt in the islands of Japan before the Japanese were the Ainus. Some attribute a Mongolian, others, especially European scholars like Bälz and Chamberlain, a Caucasian origin to the Ainus. At the present time about 17,000 Ainus live on the island of Ezo. They form a contrast to the Japanese, for they are powerfully built, exceedingly hairy, and on a lower level of civilization. It is a question whether the numerous remains of the stone age found in almost every part of the Japanese islands are to be attributed to the ancestors of these Ainus, or to a people who inhabited the land prior to the Ainus. Most scholars, especially Professor Koganei, ascribe them to the Ainus The opposite view, however, based on important grounds, is held by Professor Tsuboi of Tokio. He thinks that these ancient remains point to a people before the Ainus, who were related to the Eskimos and identical with the Korpogurus,[1] the race of dwarfs that according to the Ainu legends dwelt in the land before them.

The origin of the Japanese is also much disputed. It is certain that a race of people related to the Koreans and Manchurians, who had progressed beyond the stone age, and used weapons made of metal, gradually invaded Japan from the continent through Korea. It is possible that these invaders had some Ainu blood in them. They clearly possessed marked Malay elements. Comparative philology divides the different Mongolian nations into two groups: those whose language is analytic, and those whose language is synthetic. The Japanese with the Koreans, Manchurians, Finns and Turks belong to the latter group. In any case they stand nearer it than the Chinese and Tibetans, whose language is analytic.

The two most important sources of information for the ancient times of Japanese history are the Kojiki, i.e. chronicle of antiquity, and the Nihonshoki (abbreviated to Nihongi) i.e. written annals of Japan. The Kojiki contains merely the genealogy of the imperial family, without any chronological information. The Nihongi forms a supplement to the Kojiki; it is arranged in the form of annals after the Chinese model. The handwriting of the Kojiki is Japanese,

---

[1] Literally: people under the Indian plantain.

AINU

while that of the Nihongi is Chinese. The former was written down in 712 A.D., the latter in 720 A.D., and both are by the same author. Even for a later time, we have only contemporary information to go on. For since the author, with the exception of scattered Chinese and Korean sources which he used for the Nihongi, found his material for the earlier time solely in tradition, his information about the very earliest period is most untrustworthy. Both works, however, have a semi-official character; they were composed at the instigation of the Emperor, and thus caused the author purposely to falsify and invent in favour of the imperial dynasty.

In the opinion of Professor Yonekichi Miyake authentic history begins with Suiko-Tennō (33rd Emperor 592 B.C.—628 B.C.) and the period of the 26th Emperor Keitai-Tennō (507 B.C.—531 B.C.) stands out more clearly from the earlier legendary times, and may be compared with the dawn. It is not possible to make any sharp division between history and legend in those ancient times. Only the following facts can with certainty be regarded as historical for those early years : the unity of the imperial dynasty from the beginning of the Japanese state; wars with the savage races already settled in the islands; wars with the Koreans and the temporary overthrow of their country, and as a result, the introduction of Chinese culture and civilization. But the ancient traditions of the early period are of sufficient interest for some account of them to be given here.

FIRST PERIOD

FROM THE BEGINNING OF THE EMPIRE TO THE FALL OF THE SOGA FAMILY.

PART I

FROM THE BEGINNING OF THE EMPIRE TO THE SUBJECTION OF KOREA.

THE TEMPLE OF IZUMO-NO-OYASHIRO

Face p. 7]

CHAPTER I

FOUNDATION OF THE JAPANESE EMPIRE. THE FIRST EMPEROR

ACCORDING to the legend, the Japanese islands were created by the god Izanagi-no-Mikoto and his wife Izanami-no-Mikoto. Their daughter, Amaterasu-Omikami,[1] the sun goddess, was charitable, virtuous and clever; she taught men to cultivate the earth, to obtain silk and weave it in the loom. Her brother, Susa-noo-no-Mikoto, in contrast to her, was cruel and fierce. Therefore he was banished from Heaven to Izumo, a province on the island of Honto.[2] He built a house there, and married a beautiful girl who bore him a son named Okuninushi-no-Mikoto. He was kind, clever and brave; he defeated all the frontier tribes and encouraged agriculture. When Amaterasu-Omikami sent an ambassador to demand the whole of his kingdom, he obeyed, and at once delivered up the land. He withdrew to the village of Kizuki in the province of Izumo and dwelt there till the end

---

[1] *i.e.* the divinity that shines down from Heaven.
[2] The principal island of Japan.

of his days. There is a large temple, Izumo-no-ōyashiro, in which he is still worshipped as a god.

Amaterasu-Omikami, so the Nihongi relates, caused her grandson, Ninigi-no-Mikoto, to come down from heaven and spoke to him in these words: "Go to Japan where the meadows are green and fertile. Broad Japan shall be ruled by our descendants to all eternity, and our posterity shall endure forever like heaven and earth." She gave him Yada-no-Kagami, a mirror, Yasakani-no-Magatema, a precious stone, and Murakumo-no-Tsurugi, a sword with the words: "These insignia shall be symbols of the Imperial power, and the worthy palladia of our Empire. The mirror, especially, shall remind you of me."

Ninigi-no-Mikoto took the insignia and accompanied by many gods came down from Heaven to Hiūga, a province on the island of Kiūsiū, and ruled there. After Ninigi-no-Mikoto came in succession: his son Hikohohodemi-no-Mikoto, his grandson Ugayafukiaezu-no-Mikoto and his great-grandson Jimmu-Tennō.[1] Jimmu-Tennō is the actual founder of the Japanese Empire.

The Emperor Jimmu lived in the province of Hiūga on the island of Kiūsiū. One day he gathered together his family and his faithful adherents and said to them: "Many traitors and evil-doers live

---

[1] Tennō is a Chinese word, Ten=heaven, O=king; other epithets for the Japanese Emperor are *e.g.* Tenshi=son of heaven and Mikado (Mi=sublime, Kado gate, portal).

in the east, and they oppress, rob, and plunder our good people. Therefore we must conquer them, and protect the good people." And he set out to do so with a powerful army and with his whole family. They went through the straits of Hayasui, and the inland sea of Seto to Naniwa[1] and landed there, in order to pursue their march into the province of Yamato, which Nagasunehiko, the leader of the rebellion, was plundering. When Nagasunehiko heard of the approach of Jimmu-Tennō, he marched out to meet him, and a battle ensued on the mountain of Ikoma. In spite of great courage, the imperial army was defeated by the enemy.

The Emperor's eldest brother was mortally wounded and soon died. Jimmu-Tennō therefore abandoned the plan of reaching Yamato by land, marched back to Naniwa, and took ship to Kii, the nearest province on the sea coast to Yamato. He landed there on the shores of Kuma-no-Ura. Michinoomi-no-Mikoto, a native of the place who was a faithful servant of the Emperor, showed him the way across the mountains thought to be impassable. The imperial army conquered and brought into subjection all the rebels met on the way. When they reached Yamato, Nagasunehiko was murdered by his brother-in-law, Nigihayahi-no-Mikoto, a relative of the Emperor, who then put himself at the head of the army, and delivered it and the province of Yamato to the Emperor Jimmu.

[1] Now Osaka.

The neighbouring people of Tsuchikumo[1] were also soon brought into subjection.

After the defeat of his enemies, Jimmu-Tennō built a large palace at the foot of the mountain Unebi, and ascended the throne, 11th February, 660 B.C.

Such is the legendary account of the origin of the Imperial dynasty, and the foundation of the Japanese Empire by Jimmu-Tennō. Jimmu's personality is equally legendary. But it is certain that from the earliest times about which we possess any historical information until the present day, only one dynasty has ruled over Japan, and that the Japanese Imperial family[2] is regarded as the oldest of all reigning families.

Japanese chronology begins with 11th February, 660 B.C.,[3] the day of Jimmu-Tennō's accession.

---

[1] Tsuchi=earth, Kumo Spider. They were so named because they lived in caves.

[2] Through the great importance attached to the family in Japan, family tradition plays a prominent part. An interruption of the Imperial dynasty would have been an event of such importance that not even the vaguest tradition could have ignored it.

[3] The late Professor Naka believes that this date of the Nihongi should be put back about 660 years.

CHAPTER II

RELATIONS WITH KOREA. STRUGGLES WITH THE NATIVE RACES. STATE OF CIVILIZATION

OUR sources give no information for the next 560 years worthy of mention here. We find nothing of interest until the reign of the 10th Emperor Sujin (97-30 B.C.).

Under Sujin-Tennō the Japanese government entered into relations with Korea. The state of Karak (Mimana)[1] in the south-east of the peninsula, so the narrative runs, was oppressed by the Korean state Sil-la (Shiraki), and asked help of Sujin-Tennō. In 33 B.C. he sent a small army to its aid under Shiono-ritsuhiko-no-Mikoto who was victorious over Sil-la. The army remained in Karak, and Japan soon regarded it as a right to keep an army there permanently, and to exercise a certain authority over the state.

Besides, this successful enterprise in a foreign land, the old chroniclers tell of fierce battles fought in

---

[1] The Korean states are here given their Korean names: the Japanese names are given in brackets.

their own land against the native races which had not been entirely subdued.

In the southern part of the island of Kiūsiū in the province of Osumi, dwelt a race called Kumaso on account of its barbarity. In the time of the 12th Emperor Keikō-Tennō (71-130 A.D.) that people rebelled against the Emperor. Keikō-Tennō at first put down the rebellion. But it broke out again, and he sent his son, Prince Yamatota-keru-no-Mikoto to quell it. He was then only 15 years old. When he arrived in the province of Osumi in order to do battle with the insubordinate people, their chief was arranging a ceremony for consecrating a new palace. Yamatotakeru-no-Mikoto put on girl's dress, and mingling with the girls, entered the hall where the festival was held. He assisted in pouring out the wine, and was taken for a beautiful waiting-maid. When the chief was sunk in sleep, the Prince drew out the sword that he had concealed under his garments, and stabbed him in the back with the words : " Know, traitor, that I am the son of Keikō-Tennō, and am come here to overthrow you." The chief replied: " I am the bravest man of the west country, but you are stronger than I am, spare me, and I will bestow on you the title of honour, Yamatotakeru-no-Mikoto."[1] But the prince preferred to kill him, and ever after, peace reigned in the land.

Later the east was disturbed by the Ainus.[2] The

---

[1] *i.e.* the bravest man in Japan.

[2] Or Ezo.

rising spread as far as the plain of Kantō. Keikō-Tennō again ordered his son Yamatotakeru-no-Mikoto to put it down. First the prince went to the temple in the province of Ise in order to pray and to take with him for his protection the sword belonging to the imperial insignia. Then he marched along the shore of the Eastern Sea to Suruga where a part of the rebels opposed him. As the prince came nearer, the enemy set fire to the thick prairie grass, in order to destroy his army. But when the prince was surrounded by the flames, he mowed the grass near him with his sword,[1] and immediately a high wind sprang up which blew towards the rebels so that they perished in the flames. The prince then marched to the nearest port in the province of Sagami, and with his army embarked for the opposite province of Kazusa. On the way a storm arose and his ship was in danger of sinking. His wife, the princess Tachibanahime, in great fear, prayed to the god of the sea to still the waves. But the god caused her to sink into the water and be drowned because she had doubted his goodness. Then the sea became calm, and the army were able to land on the shore of Kazusa. Thence it continued its march to Mutsu, the chief town of the Ainus. On its arrival, the rebels submitted to the victorious general who was now able to set out on his return. He reached the province of Omi by way of Kai, Shinano and Owari. There the mountains were

---

[1] From that time the sword was named Kusanagi, *i.e.* mowing-sword.

infested by robbers, and their capture was the prince's last deed. For immediately afterwards he was attacked by an illness to which he shortly succumbed in the province of Ise. A temple was built in his honour in the province of Owari, which is now called Atsuta. The sword he had used in his last campaign was preserved there.

But these deeds of Keikō-Tennō and Prince Yamatotakeru-no-Mikoto belong rather to legend than to authentic history. The one historical fact that stands out is that for a long period after the foundation of their empire by the imperial dynasty, the Japanese had to fight with savage tribes who continually made fresh attempts to regain the liberty of which they had been deprived.

Our sources record one reform of the 11th Emperor, Suinin (29 B.C. to 70 A.D.) that has interest for the history of civilization. Until his reign it was the custom when a ruler died to bury alive with him a number of his servants, so that they might wait on him in the world beyond the grave. Suinin-Tennō made a strict law forbidding the custom for ever; for the future, instead of living men, clay figures of men, birds and horses were to be placed in the tomb.

Numerous excavations prove that the custom assigned by tradition to Suinin-Tennō was known to antiquity. It was usual also to place in the grave with the dead man the utensils he used daily, his jewels and his arms. Those objects form valuable historical documents for us, since we learn from them the conditions of civilization of the time. Men wore coats with tight sleeves and breeches, similar to European dress.[1] The materials were hemp or leather. The neck, chest, hands and loins were adorned with precious stones such as agates. The men bound up their hair like women. Great care was bestowed on the manufacture of arms; they are of excellent workmanship; iron swords, spears, arrow points and helmets have been found. The bows were made of wood, but have not been preserved. Great progress had already been made in the manufacture of pottery.

---

[1] These clothes were supplanted by Chinese dress, which later gave way again to Japanese fashions.

CHAPTER III

THE SUBJECTION OF KOREA

ACCORDING to the Nihongi chronicle the Kumaso rose in rebellion again in the time of Chūai-Tennō, (192-200 A.D.). The Emperor, accompanied by his wife, Jingū-Kōgō, marched out to subdue them. The Empress was convinced that the Kumaso were relying on the aid of the state of Sil-la in Korea, and wished to conquer that state first, for if it was once subdued, the Kumaso would soon cease to offer resistance. But the Emperor refused to follow her advice, and preferred to punish the rebellious people first. He could, however, do nothing against them; he was wounded in the battle and died soon after. The Empress concealed his death, and took counsel with the minister, Takeuchi-no-Sukune, and they determined to attack Sil-la.

At that time the peninsula of Korea consisted of four independent states, namely, Sil-la (Shiraki) in the south-east, Pak-je (Kudara) in the south-west, Ko-gu-ryu (Koma) in the north, and Karak (Mimana) situated between Pak-je and Sil-la. The earliest formation of states in Korea preceded the rise of the Japanese Empire. It goes back to the Chinese prince Ki-ja

THE SUBJECTION OF KOREA

who founded the state of Chōsun (Chōsen) in the northern part of the peninsula in 1120 with the capital Phyöng-Yang (Heijō). There soon arose three states in the southern portion of the peninsula, namely Ma-han (Bakan), Chin-han (Shinkan) and Phön-han (Benkan). The three states together were called the three Han (Kan).

Chin-han was conquered in 57 B.C. by the province named Sil-la and was thenceforward called Sil-la. Ma-han was conquered by Pak-je (18 B.C.) and received its name from that province, and in the same way Chōsun was subdued by Ko-gu-ryu (37 B.C.) and was then called after that province. The three states together are called the Postsan-han (Kan). In the same way Pyön-chin was conquered by Karak, the smallest of the states. It is related that Karak put itself under the authority of Japan in the time of Sujin-Tennō.

The Empress Jingū-Kōgō assumed man's attire and with a large army went across the Genkai Sea and the Japanese Sea to Sil-la. The king of that state was taken by surprise and surrendered after a little fighting. He offered eighty ships filled with gold, silver and silk as tribute, and promised: "I will send the same number of ships laden with treasure every year as tribute. As long as the sun rises in the east and sets in the west, as long as the river Yalu does not flow up to the mountains from the sea, I will not omit to pay the tribute." And so the Empress returned to Japan with great booty. When she landed in the province of Tsukushi, which is situated in the north of the island of Kiūsiū, she bore a son, the future Ojin-Tennō (200 A.D.) Very soon afterwards the King of Pak-je submitted and paid tribute and the King of Ko-gu-ryu followed suit.

This account in the Nihongi of the campaign of the Empress Jingū-Kōgō in Korea must certainly be regarded as legendary. But it is stated in Korean sources that there were at that time many fierce battles between Japanese and Koreans in which the Japanese gained the upper hand, and became rulers of the peninsula. We can therefore draw conclusions as to the power of the Japanese Empire and its dynasty at that time.

Japan was able to maintain its authority over Korea amid many fierce and not always successful battles, at least in some degree, until 668 A.D.

The conquest of Korea was a very important event for the Japanese people. Through Korea Japan came into relations with the highly developed civilization of China, a circumstance that had important influence in the evolution of Japanese civilization.

PART II

FROM THE INTRODUCTION OF CHINESE CULTURE
TO THE FALL OF THE SOGA FAMILY.

CHAPTER IV

THE INTRODUCTION OF CHINESE CULTURE INTO JAPAN. ECONOMIC PROGRESS OF THE NATION

CHINESE writing and literature penetrated into Japan from Korea.

According to the Nihongi chronicle, the scholars Achiki and Wani came from Pak-je. Wani brought with him the Bible of Confucius, called Rongo, and the poem Senjimon, i.e., the poem of a thousand letters, and gave it to Ojin-Tennō (201-310 A.D.). He received the two men kindly and bade them instruct the crown prince, Uji-no-Wakairatsuko, in Chinese literature. Later, a Chinaman named Achi-no-mi, came to Japan with many of his countrymen, and settled in the provinces of Kawachi and Yamato. These Chinese and Koreans and their descendants for many generations were clerks and secretaries in the service of the Japanese government. The economic life of Japan made great progress under Chinese influence. Chinese architecture was adopted from Korea, and also the production of *Saki* from rice. Chinese weavers and tailors soon came into the land and taught their industries to the Japanese.

Chinese influence doubtless improved the condition of the Japanese people and made for progress in their economic life. Tradition points at this period to the popular and happy reigns of a Nintoku-Tennō and Yūriaku-Tennō.

The Nihongi relates that the Emperor Ojin preferred his youngest son, Vji-no-Wakairatsuko to all his other children and made him crown prince instead of his eldest son, Nintoku. When on the death of his father, Wakairatsuko prepared to ascend the throne of his ancestors, his elder brother opposed him and won the support of the people. Wakairatsuko who soon saw that he would not be able to establish his claim, committed suicide. Filled with grief for his brother's fate, Nintoku-Tennō ascended the throne of his fathers and reigned with wisdom and mercy (313-399 A.D.). He restored the palace at Naniwa. When he became acquainted with the poverty of the people, he had pity on them and exempted them from the payment of taxes for three years. And so it happened that the Emperor became poor and could not repair the walls and roof of his palace. But he thought only of the welfare of his subjects, and when the Empress complained of their poverty, replied: " I feel joy and sorrow with my people, if they become richer then also shall I become richer."

It is told that the Emperor Yūriaku (457-479 A.D), sent ambassadors to the south of China, and had women weavers and tailors brought thence that they might teach the Japanese their industries. And the Japanese began to weave brocade and silk damask and to do artistic embroidery. The Empress herself bred silk-worms as an example for the people. The Emperor encouraged the immigration of makers of porcelain, potters, and coiners from Pak-je. The Japanese proved apt pupils, and Chinese fashions in architecture and industrial arts made great progress in the land.

CHAPTER V

THE REBELLION OF KOREA

IN the time of the 21st Emperor, Yūriaku, a Japanese commander in Karak on the peninsula of Korea, named Kibi-no-Tasa, allied himself with the King of Sil-la. He was really a vassal of the Japanese Empire, but he had great power at his command, and strove after independence. At first the Emperor wished to proceed there in person and punish the traitor, but by the request and advice of his councillors he gave up the plan, and commanded his general, Ki-no-Oyumi, to undertake the campaign. He had little success and fell in battle.

During the reign of the 23rd Emperor, Kenzo-Tennō (485-487 A.D.), Oiwa, the son of the Japanese general, Ki-no-Oyumi, revolted in Korea. He wished to make himself king over the three Han, and conspired with the King of Ko-gu-ryu. But the army of the state of Pak-je which remained loyal, attacked him and compelled him to flee to the north.

Later, under the 26th Emperor, Keitai (507-531 A.D.), the state of Karak revolted when at the wish of the King of Pak-je, the Chancellor Otomo-no-

THE REBELLION OF KOREA

Kanamura agreed to surrender a part of Karak. Soon after, the King of Sil-la allied himself with a Japanese Kuni-no-miyatsuko[1] named Iwai and conquered a part of Karak. The Emperor commanded his general, Mononobe-no-Arakahi, to destroy Iwai and then to subdue Sil-la.

In the time of the 29th Emperor, Kimmei (540-571 A.D.), Sil-la undertook an invasion of Pak-je. Seimei-ō, king of that province, fell in battle. Sil-la's troops went against Karak, and drove out the Japanese commander (562 A.D.). The Emperor sent an army against Sil-la, but it was defeated in a fierce battle. Karak was now completely subdued by Sil-la, and the Japanese rule was not again restored there. The Japanese authority was maintained only in Pak-je and Ko-gu-ryu.

In spite, however, of all the blood spilled by Japan in upholding its power in Korea, and the decrease of that power, the march of civilization induced by the conquest of that land, continued its steady progress. It showed itself especially in that the religion prevailing on the continent was introduced into Japan.

We have already mentioned in the introduction that from about the time of the 26th Emperor, the matter of our sources becomes more trustworthy, and that from the reign of Suiko-Tennō, we have real authentic history. The information about the introduction of Buddhism into Japan may be regarded as absolutely trustworthy.

[1] Overseer of a province.

CHAPTER VI

THE BEGINNINGS OF BUDDHISM IN JAPAN

THE Japanese, like the Aryan races, in the beginning worshipped the forces of nature as divine beings, e.g. the sun as Amaterasu-Omikami, who was regarded as the mother from whom the imperial family sprang. Side by side with the worship of the forces of nature was the worship of ancestors. Ancestor-worship is closely connected with the important position occupied by the head of the family among the ancient Japanese. After his death the father of the family enjoyed divine honours. Each family regarded its own ancestors as gods, and all the Japanese worshipped the dead Emperor and various heroes as gods. Every year a festival was celebrated in honour of the ancestors. It was believed that on that day the ancestors came down into the houses of their descendants and wandered about among them. The people bathed, and put on their best garments on that day, kindled lights, placed food for the ancestors and devoted the day to their memory.

Buddhism came into successful rivalry with this ancient Kami-worship,[1] but the old religious views

[1] Kami = ancestors.

BEGINNINGS OF BUDDHISM IN JAPAN

were never entirely suppressed. Buddhism indeed was comparatively tolerant to them. At the present time the old ancestor-worship is continued in the so-called Shintoism, which experienced a revival in the 18th century on the awakening of imperialist convictions.

In the time of the Emperor Keita, a Chinese named Shiba-Tatto brought an image of Buddha with him, and settled in Japan. But he was not able to convert any Japanese to his faith.

In 552 A.D., Kimmei-Tennō, the King of Pak-je sent over the image of Buddha and sacred Buddhist books. The Emperor asked his two highest officers of state, O-omi and O-muraji, whether Buddha should be believed in or not.

Now bitter enmity prevailed between O-omi and O-muraji, the heads of two rival groups of families. O-omi (i.e. Great Omi) was chief of the Omi family to which Soga, Heguri, and Katsuragi belonged. They were descended from the family of the Takeuchi, who with the Empress Jingū-Kōgō had subdued Korea. They possessed by inheritance one of the two offices of chancellor. The two Muraji families, the Mononobe and Nakatomi possessed the other, and so they each strove for the chief power in the Empire. The attitude of the two high officials towards Buddhism corresponded to the enmity between the two families. O-omi, named Soga-no-Iname, made this reply to the Emperor's question: "Buddhism is a sublime spiritual religion, and therefore all cizilized peoples accept it." O-Muraji, named Mononobe-no-Okoshi, replied on the contrary: "We shall remain true to our old religion, otherwise the gods will chastise us." The Emperor delivered the image and the sacred books to O-omi, and said: "You, only, believe in him, and leave the people to their old faith." Soga-no-Iname rejoiced over those words, pulled down his house and on its site built a temple to Buddha in which he worshipped him every day.

Soon after the plague broke out, and Mononobe-no-Okoshi assured the Emperor that it was a punishment sent by the gods for O-omi's conversion to the new religion. With the Emperor's permission he burnt O-omi's temple, and threw the image of Bhudda into the pond Naniwa in the province of Yamato. Henceforth the enmity between the two families was greatly increased; it was inherited by their sons and by all the families related to them and their vassals. The army, also, which gave allegiance to both families, divided into two parties, and at last things went so far that Moriya, the son of Mononobe-no-Okoshi, and Umako, the son of Soga-no-Iname made war on each other. The Mononobe family was conquered in a fierce battle, and entirely destroyed by the Soga family which adhered to Buddhism. The holding of high office of any O-Muraji was made impossible for ever by the destruction of the Mononobe. This happened in the reign of Jōmei-Tennō (585-587 A.D.). Religion had not been the principal cause of the fighting. Peace could not have lasted long between the two powerful officials, O-omi and O-Muraji: A decisive battle between them was inevitable. The religious question which had then become acute was mingled with the rivalry of the two high officials. The Soga family who had declared in favour of the new religion were the conquerors. Thus Buddhism would be accepted in the official class.

CHAPTER VII

THE REGENCY OF THE CROWN PRINCE SHOKOTU. DIRECT INTERCOURSE WITH CHINA. FURTHER INTRODUCTION OF CHINESE CULTURE AND OF BUDDHISM.

AFTER the murder of the Emperor Sushūn (587-592 A.D.) by the chancellor, Umako, his sister, Suiko-Tennō (592-628 A.D.) ascended the throne as first Empress. The crown prince, later called Shōtoku,[1] conducted the government for her as regent. He was an enlightened adherent of Chinese culture. He tried to promote learning in Japan through alliance with China. He began to form the administration of home affairs on the Chinese model. He decreed that the officials should wear a uniform, which should distinguish them from the common people, and also mark their rank, and tried to awake in them a strict consciousness of duty. The 17 articles dealing with morals issued by him under the title of "Constitution" were especially directed to the official class.

---

[1] During his life-time his name was Umayadono-Oji or Toyoto Mimi. Shōtoku-Taishi is his posthumous title of honour, and means the greatly wise and virtuous crown prince.

REGENCY OF CROWN PRINCE SHOKOTU

The introduction of the Chinese calendar was also due to him.

He sent a Japanese ambassador to the Chinese Emperor to deliver a letter in which he invited friendly intercourse between the two nations. The ambassador was accompanied by a number of Japanese students. At that time, 589-617 A.D., the Sui dynasty was reigning in China. Under it art, learning and politics made great progress, and reached their zenith under the Tang dynasty (618-906). As those Japanese remained in China until that period, all the great results of Chinese culture were made directly accessible to Japan. The Emperor of China on his part sent an ambassador with a reply to the Empress (607 A.D.). Such was the first official political act between the two states, although private intercourse had already prevailed for a long time.

Shōtoku-Taishi embraced the Buddhist religion, and built many temples to Buddha, especially the Temples of Hōriūji[1] and Shitennōji, which are preserved to this day.

Professor C. Itō has devoted a careful study to the architecture of the temple of Hōriūji. He finds the Indian, Chinese and Greek styles in the building. The pillars of the outer gate are partly Doric, other parts, for example the roof, the windows and the galleries, are Chinese, while the interior is Indian in style. It is recognised that under Alexander the Great, Greek culture penetrated to India (327 B.C.),

---

[1] Ji = Buddhist Temple.

and it must be admitted that Indian art when it was introduced into China possessed Greek elements. The Temple of Hōriūji offers a rich field for the history of Japanese art. It contains many statues of Buddha, some in wax, others in bronze, or carved in wood. The style is called after the temple, the Hōriūji style, or after its creator, the Tori style. The walls of the temple are decorated with large portraits of Buddha. They were painted by the Buddhist priest, Donchō of Korea, who first introduced painters' colours, paper and Indian ink into Japan. The temple also contained embroideries on silk, Buddhist vessels and Chinese musical instruments which belong to that period.

CHAPTER VIII

THE FALL OF THE SOGA FAMILY

CHINESE civilization soon got a strong hold in the Japanese islands. The industrial and intellectual life of the Japanese people already bore its mark, and Buddhism steadily gained ground. But there was one fundamental difference between Japan and China, and that lay in the system of government of each state. In China an admirable system of administration had been developed, carried out in an almost modern fashion by a class of officials who, now, at the beginning of the brilliant epoch of the Tang dynasty won universal admiration. In Japan, on the contrary, the old patriarchal system of government still prevailed.

It must therefore be pointed out what an important part the family (Uji) played in the life of the Japanese nation. The Japanese family stood in intimate relation with the father of the family. The eldest son inherited the position of father of the family, and he possessed the same power over the families of his brothers and sisters as over his own children. So there was close interdependence among individual families, and family dependence and membership was of the greatest importance. The family which possessed the greatest number of kinsfolk possessed also the greatest power in the state. The most powerful families had hereditary rights to the highest offices. As the Emperor held his power through his birth and the position of his family, so the chancellors, the highest officials and the governors of the provinces held their offices through their birth and their families.[1] They did not owe their offices to the favour of the Emperor, they inherited them as the property of their family.

It can be gathered from this how little real power the Emperor had in the administration of his empire. The powerful family of the Soga, especially after the destruction of their rivals, the Mononobe, succeeded in gaining such a strong position that it could venture to defy the imperial family and even to strive after the imperial dignity. The more oppressively powerful the position of this family became, the more did the friends and representatives of the imperial dynasty feel that the government of the Japanese state must be reformed after the Chinese model.

The crown prince Shōtoku died before he succeeded to the throne. Shortly after, the chancellor, Soga-no-

[1] There were 3 classes of families: 1. The Kōbetsu, families of the imperial race. To those belonged e.g. the Soga. 2. The Shimbetsu, families of the Emperor's vassals. To those belonged e.g. the Nakatomi. 3. The Hambetsu, the families of Chinese and Korean immigrants.

Umako, who had been a champion of Buddhism also died. His son, Emishi, inherited his office. He arrogated to himself more independence than his father had had, and appointed his son Iruka to sit in office with him without the Emperor's permission. Iruka was cruel, and more arrogant and overbearing than his father. He designated his son by the title of prince and called his house the imperial court. At last he set aside the sons of the crown prince Shōtoku with their families, and thought thereby to destroy the imperial dynasty for ever.

But there was a noble at the imperial court, by name Nakatomi-no-Kamatari, who was faithful to the imperial family and sought to bring about the downfall of the Soga family. For that purpose he took counsel with the wise prince, Naka-no-ōe-Oji, and they decided on the murder of the arrogant chancellor. It was not merely an act of vengeance, a great political idea was allied with it: to administer the government of the Japanese Empire on the Chinese pattern. Both had studied the Chinese form of government, and had long had it in mind to introduce into Japan a number of ministers and officials as was the case in China. To carry out the plan, it was first necessary to destroy the Soga family.

During the festival at which the Korean ambassadors offered tribute to Kōgioku-Tennō (642-645 A.D.), they murdered the Chancellor Iruka at the feet of the Empress, and had his palace surrounded by their faithful adherents. Emishi, surprised, burnt all the treasures and documents of the state, among them the oldest historical works of Japan.[1] Then he, together with the remaining members of his family, sought death in the flames (645 A.D.).

With the fall of the Soga family the last obstacle to the complete adoption of Chinese civilisation was removed. The government of the Japanese empire could now be modelled on the Chinese plan, and in place of the old patriarchal government arose a much more modern system.

---

[1] The Tennō-ki and the Koku-ki which were written before the Nihongi in 720. The Kuji-ki which was long regarded as a part of the Koku-ki that had been preserved, is a later forgery.

SECOND PERIOD

FROM THE TAIKA REFORMS TO THE FALL OF
THE TAIRA FAMILY.

PART I

FROM THE TAIKA REFORMS TO THE FOUNDA-
TION OF THE CAPITAL, KIOTO.

CHAPTER I

THE TAIKA REFORMS

Soon after the violent end of the arrogant Chancellor and his family, the Empress abdicated in favour of her brother, who ascended the throne as Kōtoku-Tennō (645-654 A.D.). He immediately gave the chief authors of the great revolution, Prince Naka-no-ōe-Oji and Nakatomi-no-Kamatori, an important part in the management of the administration. He also appointed as his advisers Takamuko-no-Kuromaro and Sōbin, two men who had lived in China for a long time and were intimately acquainted with Chinese literature, and especially with the political administrative conditions of that country; with their aid he began to reform the government and administration of his Empire according to the Chinese model. The great significance of the reform received outward expression by the introduction of the Chinese custom of giving a name to the years, and so those years were called Taika, i.e. great reformation.

Instead of the high officers of state who owed their dignities to family descent, officials were now appointed whose posts were not hereditary. The great plenipotentiaries in the provinces were set aside, and replaced by governors who were immediately dependent on the crown, and were changed every four years, so that they might not seek after independent power. Every province was declared to be the property of the Emperor, and all inhabitants the subjects of the crown; they had no longer to pay the taxes to the governor of the province, but direct to the state itself. The officials, unlike the former plenipotentiaries, received a salary. According to a census taken at that time, every man received two Tan[1] of rice-fields, and every woman two-thirds of a Tan. On the death of the owner the land was to go back to the government. Every man had to pay a fixed annual tribute of rice, each family an annual tax of part of the produce of their land according to its extent, e.g. fruit, silk, or fish. Every man between 20 and 50 years of age was obliged to work 10 days in each year for the government, but he could get exemption from that duty by paying in kind. The Emperor made roads and kept post horses in the towns and villages in order to facilitate communication with the provinces, and to preserve better control over the administration.

---

[1] A Tan = about 1200 square yards of land.

CHAPTER II

THE AINU INSURRECTION. END OF JAPANESE RULE IN KOREA. CONTINUATION OF REFORM

AFTER the death of Kōtoku-Tennō, his sister, Kōgioku-Tennō, ascended the throne for the second time under the name of Saimei-Tennō (655-661 A.D.). The crown prince Naka-no-ōe-Oji assisted her in the execution of her duties without assuming the imperial dignity.

At that time there was an insurrection of the Ainus. The Empress commissioned the general, Abe-no-Hirafu to put it down, and he succeeded in accomplishing the difficult task. The Mishihase or Makkatsu who also rebelled soon after were subdued by him. But the government were not able to cope with the disturbance in Korea which through the encroachment of China now entered on a new phase.

For the last hundred years there had been continual fighting between the states of the peninsula of Korea. As related above, Sil-la had fallen off from Japan, and submitted to the province of Karak. Only Pak-je and Ko-gu-ryu recognised the authority of Japan. When at this time Sil-la again fought with

Pak-je, it asked help of the imperial dynasty, Tang, in China. Chinese troops joined with the army of Sil-la and invaded Pak-je. The auxiliary troops sent by Japan defeated the Chinese army after severe fighting. Saimei-Tennō died at that time, and the crown prince, Naka-no-ōe-Oji ascended the throne as Tenji-Tennō (668-671 A.D.). As the Chinese now succeeded in subduing Ko-gu-ryu, and so bringing the whole of the peninsula under their rule, Tenji-Tennō gave up resistance. Sil-la gained all the conquered territory, but was compelled to recognise Chinese supremacy (668 A.D.). So ended Japanese rule in Korea. It had cost Japan much blood without bringing any lasting political advantage. Its chief importance lies in its influence on civilization.

Tenji-Tennō made the town of Shiga on the banks of the lake of Biwa in the province of Omi his place of residence. With exceeding energy he continued the task of reforming domestic administration. He founded schools, and enacted that a census of the people should be taken regularly every five years, and made many other laws and decrees. On that account he was called the "Restorer."

Under Tenji-Tennō, Nakatomino-Kamatari, the man who had played so important a part in the destruction of the Soga and in the new reforms, enjoyed great honour. He was Tenji-Tennō's right hand and confidential minister. When he was dangerously ill, the Emperor visited him at his own house, and bestowed on him the title of Taishokukan, which signified great distinction, and the family name of

Fujiwara. After Kamatari's death the temple of Tō-no-mine was built in his honour, in which, even to-day, divine honours are paid him. Hence came the rise of the Fujiwara family which later played so important a part.

Tenji-Tennō was succeeded by his son Kōbun-Tennō (672 A.D.). But after three months he was attacked by Prince Oama, Tenji-Tennō's brother, a personal enemy of Tenji-Tennō, at the head of a large army, and therefore committed suicide. Oama ascended the throne under the title of Temmu-Tennō (672-686 A.D.). Although hitherto hostile to Tenji-Tennō he accepted his reforms, and to some extent carried them further.

CHAPTER III

REFORMS OF THE FIRST TAIHO YEAR

A SECOND epoch of reform was inaugurated by the reign of the 42nd Emperor, Mommu (696-707 A.D.), the grandson of Temmu-Tennō. Under his rule, Prince Osakabe and the minister, Fujiwara Fubito, son of the famous minister, Kamatari, in the first Taihō year added a number of laws and decrees after the Chinese model to the reforms of Kōto-ku-Kuno and Tenji-Tennō (701 A.D.), reforms which, except for slight changes, remained valid until modern times.

According to this new arrangement the two Kan, Jingikan and Dajōkan formed the central points of the government. The care of the ancient religious belief and ancestor-worship was entrusted to the Jingikan. The Dajōkan consisted of a group of three persons, namely, the Chief Chancellor (Dajōdaijin) the Chancellor of the Left (Sadajin), and the Chancellor of the Right (Udaijin). They were assisted by eight ministers, viz., Nakatsukasa, the chief minister, whose duty was to write down and proclaim all the edicts of the Emperor; Shikibu, who was master of the ceremonies and minister of public worship and instruction;

REFORMS OF THE FIRST TAIHO YEARS

Jibu, overseer of the officials working in the provinces; Minbu, minister of commerce and agriculture; Hiōbu, minister of war; Kiōbu, minister of justice; Okura, minister of finance; and Kunai, minister of buildings and works in the imperial palace. The Dajōkan were also assisted by the Dainagon,[1] who lived in close attendance on the Emperor as advisers and monitors; and the Dainagon were again assisted by the Shōnagon.[2] Later on the Dainagon succeeded in making their close relations with the Emperor of great importance. Together with the Chūnagon,[3] they formed a council called Sangi.

The capital was divided into two districts. The Kiōshiki stood at the head of each of those districts, and the Kokuji at the head of the provinces, below them came the Gunji. Those officials, as stated above, were changed every four years. The province of Tsukushi, in the north of the island of Kiūsiū which was of especial importance for the defence of the frontier against China and Korea, was administered by a council, "Dazaifu," which besides the duties of a prefect had also military powers for the purpose of securing the safety of the frontier. The province of Settsu with the important port of Naniwa (now Osaka) was administered by a Settsu-shiki which also had to look after the building of ships and the carrying on of trade.

---

[1] Dai = great, Nagon = monitor.
[2] Shō = small.
[3] Chū = middle.

There was a university in the capital and a school in each province. The imperial guard was quartered in the capital and an army corps was kept in each province.

The criminal code contained five different penalties: flogging with the whip; flogging with the stick; banishment to another province; banishment to a distant island; and death.

The carrying out of these reforms on the Chinese model cut so deeply into the old conditions of government that an admirable modern state was created out of the old patriarchal form of government.

The great political progress, the formation of a complicated official system and the relations into which the state had entered with China, demanded a permanent seat of government which had hitherto been lacking. It had been the custom to change the seat of government with almost every new sovereign. But there was soon to be an end of that system.

CHAPTER IV

THE SEVEN COURTS OF NARA. BUDDHISM, ART AND LEARNING.

MOMMU-TENNO left a son who was a minor, and so his mother ascended the throne in his place under the name of Gemmiō-Tennō (707-715 A.D.). She built a palace in the Chinese style at Nara, and placed the seat of government there, and seven Emperors resided there one after the other: Gemmiō, Genshō (715-724 A.D.), Shōmu (724-749), Kōken (749-758), Jūnnin (758-764), Shōtoku (764-769), and Kōnin (769-781 A.D.). This period of the history of Japan is called "the seven courts of Nara," a time when Chinese influence held full sway.

Gemmiō-Tennō was the first to introduce bronze coinage into Japan, and as in China, each coin had a square hole in the middle.

To her also we owe the earliest source of Japanese history that has come down to us. She ordered the Kojiki to be written down by a nobleman at the court, named O-no-Yasumaro, and it was finished in 722. It covers the period from the beginning of Japanese history to the time of the Empress Suiko (592-628 A.D.). It was based on the oral statements of Hieda-no-Ares, an imperial vassal who owed his information to Temmu-Tennō. By her order, also, a topographical description of the provinces, called Fudoki, was made. During the reign of the next Empress, Genshō-Tennō, O-no-Yasumaro, at the invitation of Prince Toneri, wrote the annals called Nihon Shoki, which are based on Chinese sources and cover the period from the origin of the Japanese Empire to Jidō-Tennō (690-696 A.D.).

Chinese influence, which entirely prevailed at this era, greatly furthered the spread of Buddhism. Shomu-Tennō, (724-749 A.D.), the successor of Genshō-Tennō, and also his wife, Kōmiō-kōgō, the daughter of the minister, Fubito, and so the first Empress not of imperial descent, were ardent adherents of the new religion. The Buddhist priesthood now began to appear at court. The Emperor regarded himself as a Buddhist monk, and called himself a servant of Buddha, a servant of the Buddhist priests and of the Buddhist doctrine. The Empress, from a sense of piety, founded a workhouse and a hospital. The Emperor built many Buddhist temples in Nara, and ordered two temples to be erected in each province, one for priests, and the other for priestesses.

The Buddhist priests, whose number increased with extraordinary rapidity, soon acquired great secular power. Many of them wholly abandoned their religious ideals, and gave themselves up to worldly interests. One of them named Dōkiō became the favourite of the Empress Kōken, and succeeded in attaining great power at court. If he did not actually possess the title of Chief Chancellor, he was the real leader of the government. His ambition even soared as high as the imperial dignity itself. Wake-no-Kiyomaro, who warned the Empress of the priest's plans, was banished from the court for his information, and only after the death of the Empress was Dōkiō exiled for life to the province of Shimozuke by her successor.

The most important of the Buddhist temples of that time was Tōdaiji in Nara. It is famous for its enormous gold and bronze bust of Buddha, over 48 feet high, called Nara-no-Daibutsu. There only remains of the ancient temple a subsidiary building called Shōsōin in which were preserved a number of old paintings, woven stuffs, silk embroideries, musical instruments, gold, silver and ivory vessels and cups belonging to the imperial family. The objects prove the height to which art had risen at that time. The style of the art of the period is called the Tempiō style after the name of the years in which it flourished

Distinguished scholars and authors belong also to that epoch. We may mention here Abe-no-Nakamaro and Kibi-no-Makibi, who had lived a long time in China, and were acquainted with Chinese writers like Rihaku and Toho. Nakamaro, at the request of the Emperor of China, remained in China till his death. Kibi-no-Makibi returned to Japan after 19 years absence, and became tutor to the Empress Kōken, the daughter of Shomu-Tennō and later Chancellor of the Right. He invented the Japanese syllabic writing, consisting of 50 letters arranged in tabular form, known as the Katakana.[1] The form is essentially influenced by the Sanskrit. Celebrated song-writers were Kakino-moto-no-Hitomaro and Yamabe-no-Akahito, etc. The most important collection of songs of that epoch is the Manniōshū.

---

[1] Kata = the halves, *i.e.* Makibi used halves of Chinese signs for representing the Japanese syllables. Kana = equivalent names.

CHAPTER V

FOUNDATION OF THE TOWN OF KIOTO. THE GREAT PERIOD OF LEARNING, AND FURTHER PROGRESS OF BUDDHISM.

THE 50th Emperor Kammu (781-806 A.D.), the successor of Kōnin, was not satisfied with Nara as a place of residence. He laid out a large, regular, modern city on the plan of Chang-an, the capital of the Chinese Empire and named it Heiankiō, i.e., the town of peace. Later on it was named only Kiōto, i.e., Metropolis. It continued to be the residence of the Emperor until 1869.

From the time of Gemmiō-Tennō, the Ainu tribes had been in a continual state of rebellion. All attempts to subdue them permanently had failed. Kammu-Tennō now sent the famous General Saka-none-no-Tamuramaro against them. He was a severe but just and well-meaning man. The strictest discipline prevailed in his army which was entirely devoted to him. After a long struggle he succeeded in subduing the Ainus for ever.

Shortly after the death of Kammu-Tennō disputes arose about the succession. Heijei-Tennō, who succeeded him (806-809), soon abdicated, and his brother

Saga-Tennō (809-823) ascended the throne. But Kusuko the favourite wife of Heijei-Tennō quarrelled with Saga-Tennō. She and her brother were the leaders of a conspiracy, the aim of which was to thrust Saga-Tennō from the throne, and to restore Heijei-Tennō. The conspiracy was discovered. Kusuko committed suicide, and her brother was executed.

In order to prevent such events in the future, the Emperor instituted a guard of police for the capital, and placed a body-guard about his own person, the Kebiishi.

This Emperor erected a building called Kurōdodo-koro for the preservation of documents of state. He revised the laws and ordinances of the Taihōriō.

He was a very learned man and practised the rare and highly esteemed art of writing.[1] He was also the author of valuable works; he encouraged learning and the arts, and they made great progress in his reign.

Besides the university in the capital, and the schools in the provinces, there were many private schools for the nobility, e.g., the school Gakkanin for the Tachibana family, Kangakuin for the Fujiwara family, Shōgakuin for the imperial family. Among the celebrated scholars of the time Miyako-no-Yoshika, Omi-no-Mifune and Ono-no-Takamura deserve mention.

[1] Besides the Emperor there were at that time only two men who could write, Kūkai and Tachiba-na-no-Hayanari, whose writing was for a long time typical. The three men were called Sampitsu (Sam=three, Hitsu or Pitsu=caligraphers).

FOUNDATION OF THE TOWN OF KIOTO

Saichō and Kūkai were the most distinguished of the Buddhist priests. Saichō was with the Japanese embassy to China for about a year, and on his return introduced into Japan the teaching of the Tendai, a sect widely spread through China which strove to raise the position of the priesthood both spiritually and morally. After his death he received the title of Dengiō-Daishi. The temple built by him on the hill of Hiei was the principal temple of his sect. Kūkai also went to China. On his return to Japan he spread the teaching of the Shingonshū,[1] and built a temple on the summit of the hill Kōya called Kongōbuji. Both men were distinguished for their wide culture and learning. Among other things Kūkai improved the Japanese syllabic writing and arranged it in alphabetical form. Kūkai's 47 letters are called Hirakana. After his death he received the title of honour, Kōbō Daishi.

The spread of Buddhism in Japan was greatly promoted by these two men, and especially through their toleration. They tried to reconcile Buddhism with the old Japanese faith in gods, and in ancestor-worship. They did not desire that the ancient faith should be discarded, and were content that Buddha should be worshipped side by side with the old gods, as an equally privileged god. And so it often happened at that period that a temple of the old Kami worship was joined to a Buddhist temple. The imperial court where many converts were made to Buddhism celebrated a Buddhist service.

[1] Shū = Sect.

PART II

THE AGE OF THE FUJIWARA

CHAPTER VI

THE INCREASING POWER OF THE FUJIWARA

THE leading idea in the political reforms of the Taika years had been to secure the Emperor powerful influence through the right of appointing and dismissing officials. But in spite of the fact that these reforms greatly changed the ancient procedure, hereditary and family rights and privileges played so large a part in Japan, that new independent power arose. High officials succeeded in securing their posts to members of their family; in fact appointment to office was not made for personal qualifications but on account of family descent. Thus the family of Nakatomi-no-Kamatari on whom Tenji-Tennō had bestowed the title of honour of Fujiwara, attained to very great power, and its members were continually appointed to the highest offices, and the proceeding caused many disputes and disturbances in the imperial family. Yoshifusa, the daughter of the minister Fujiwara, was the wife of Prince Michiyasu[1] and became Empress at his accession, a fact of great importance to the Fujiwara family. Through this con-

[1] After his accession he was called Montoku-Tennō.

nection with the imperial family, the Fujiwara secured the precedence of all the rest of the rival families. For future Emperors would be of their blood.

The son of the Empress belonging to the Fujiwara, was only 9 years old when, as Seiwa-Tennō (858-876) he ascended the throne. Therefore his grandfather, Fujiwara Yoshifusa, was appointed his guardian. Later on when a more youthful Emperor, Yōzei-Tennō ascended the throne, Mototsune, an adopted son of Fujiwara Yoshifusa, was appointed guardian. As Yōzei-Tennō had feeble health and was incapable of governing, Fujiwara Mototsune remained guardian when the Emperor was grown up. Mototsune greatly distinguished himself during his regency, and became so powerful that he deposed Yōzei-Tennō, and set Kōkō-Tennō (884-887) on the throne, who, being Emperor only in name, left all power and authority to Mototsune. After 5 years Kōkō-Tennō abdicated in favour of his son, Uda-Tennō (887-897). Although he was 28 years of age, Mototsune assumed the office of guardian, for so far had it come that even an Emperor who was of age had to acknowledge an officially recognised guardian from the all-powerful minister's family. Such a guardian for an adult Emperor held the title of **Kambaku**.

SUGAWARA MICHIZANE
CHANCELLOR OF THE RIGHT

CHAPTER VII

FUTILE ATTEMPTS TO DESTROY THE POWER OF THE FUJIWARA. ART AND LEARNING OF THE PERIOD

IT was natural that an Emperor, conscious in some degree of his own powers, should dislike such a guardianship, and so Uda-Tennō made an attempt to destroy the supremacy of the Fujiwara. When his Kambaku, Mototsune, died, he refused to recognise the new guardian appointed by the Fujiwara. Moreover, he sought to set up in power and esteem another family, the Sugawara, as rivals to the Fujiwara, and he appointed Michizane, a clever member of the Sugawara, Chancellor of the Right. But Uda-Tennō was not the man wholly to carry out his great political ideas for, devoted to Buddhism with his whole soul, he abdicated in favour of his twelve year old son, shaved his head, and became a Buddhist monk. He arranged that no Fujiwara should receive the office of guardian to the boy Emperor, Daigo-Tennō (897-930 A.D.), and out of hatred to them he offered Michizane the post of guardian to the young Emperor. But the power of the Fujiwara was still exceedingly great, and Michizane refused the invitation from fear of them. Mototsune's son, Fujiwara Tokihira, who was Chancellor of the Left, gained so great an influence over the young Emperor that he succeeded in slandering Michizane to him and procuring his banishment. Michizane died in exile.

When Daigo-Tennō was grown up, he ruled with wisdom and mercy. His reign lasted 33 years and was prosperous and happy. Poetry and science flourished, and the scholars and writers, Sugawara Michizane, Miyoshi Kiyoyuki and Kino Haseo, who had all had a Chinese education deserve mention. Kino Tsurayuki and Oshikōchi Mitsune were distinguished song-writers; Kino Tsurayuki wrote Japanese prose in his descriptions of travel. At the command of Daigo-Tennō they both collected Japanese songs; their comprehensive collection fills 20 volumes and is the first made with imperial co-operation.

There was also at this time a celebrated painter, named Kose Kanaoka.

CHAPTER VIII

THE BEGINNINGS OF THE FEUDAL SYSTEM

THE founding of a fixed place of residence, and the increase of prosperity resulted in more luxurious ways at court. The nobles and their families who lived at Kiōto vied with each other in the display of splendour and luxury. Many families who hitherto had held a high position lost their wealth through their extravagant way of life. On the other hand the Fujiwara, through their alliance with the imperial family, attained greater power than ever. Their supremacy was so oppressive to the other families that they preferred to leave Kiōto and settle in the country. The Fujiwara family who now held sway alone in the capital, led a life of magnificence and luxury. In the administration of the land they no longer considered the welfare of the state, but thought of their own advantage, especially of obtaining means for their luxurious way of life. They granted privileges to the officials and nobility in the provinces in return for others granted to themselves. The ordinances of the great Reform era were set aside, and official posts became hereditary. Thus the territorial nobility again became powerful, they gained extensive landed property, forced the peasants to serve them, and so were in a position to raise troops and command great military power.

This military and feudal nobility now beginning to make itself felt in the country, was later called Buke, to distinguish it from the court nobility which was called Kuge.

The development of feudalism and of the power of the nobility was closely associated with numerous internal struggles.

In the time of Suzaku-Tennō (930-946 A.D.), Taira Masakado, a descendant of Kammu-Tennō, asked the minister Fujiwara Tadahira to appoint him Colonel of the Police (Kebüshi). When Fujiwara refused, he went back to his native province of Shimōsa which lay to the east, collected troops, attacked the neighbouring province of Hidachi, and murdered the prefect who was his uncle. The central power was not strong enough to put down the rebel, who later marched through the country plundering as he went. In 939 A.D. he even built a fortress in the village of Sashiura, in the province of Shimōsa, and ruled there like an independent prince, from time to time renewing his raids into the neighbouring district. At that time also Fujiwara Sumitomo rebelled in western Japan. He allied himself with pirates, ruled the Seto inland sea with them, and made raids on the coasts. He even extended his plundering enterprises as far as the capital, Kiōto, and set fire to it.

BEGINNINGS OF THE FEUDAL SYSTEM

So that anarchical conditions prevailed. The imperial court lived in fear and terror. They managed to equip an expedition against Taira Masakado, but it only reached Shimōsa when Masakado had already been defeated and killed (940 A.D.) by independent nobles in the province of Hidachi, by Taira Sadamori, whose father he had murdered, and by Fujiwara Hidesato. Fujiwara Sumitomo, likewise, was not conquered by the central government but by the territorial nobility. His conquerors were Minamoto Tsune-moto and Ono-no-Yoshifuru.

The authority and influence of the Taira and the Minamoto greatly increased during this period. There existed a great distinction between them and the Fujiwara. The Fujiwara were a family of ministers and their importance lay in the fact that they held the court and all the officials in their hands. The others relied on the military power which they had established in their territories.

CHAPTER IX

THE FUJIWARA FAMILY AS GUARDIANS OF THE STATE. JAPANESE INFLUENCE ON CHINESE CIVILIZATION

MURAKAMI-Tennō (946-967), the son of Daigo-Tennō made a fresh attempt to get the government of the state into his own hands. Although possessed of undoubted talent, he was not successful in effecting any real reform in the conditions of government. The power of the Fujiwara family had already become too strong. His son, Reizei-Tennō (967-969), came again under the guardianship of the powerful clan, and for more than a century, the old imperial family sank into entire insignificance. The court life of the Fujiwara was of great magnificence, especially that of Fujiwara Michinaga, who governed the country for about 30 years as guardian for three Emperors. He married his three daughters to imperial princes and became the grandfather of three Emperors. His five sons were appointed to the highest offices. He set up and deposed Emperors at pleasure. The Fujiwara loved splendour and luxury and encouraged the fine arts.

Fujiwara Michinaga erected magnificent buildings and laid out fine gardens. Of all the temples he built, the finest was the royal temple at Midō. He was therefore called Midō Kambaku. His motto was: "The moon changes every month, but I am always the full moon." His son Yorimichi was also guardian for about 50 years and for three Emperors. Then he resigned and lived in royal splendour in Uji as Uji-Kambaku.

The most important circumstance of this period of the supremacy of the Fujiwara was that the Chinese civilization that had hitherto prevailed took on more and more of Japanese colour. For a long time China had been in a disturbed condition, and endless civil wars had rendered regular diplomatic intercourse with a foreign state impossible. Therefore by the advice of the chancellor, Sugawara Michizane, Daigo-Tennō had not sent ambassadors to China, and in the following years official relations had been lacking with a country torn by civil war. So that Japanese civilization began to assume an independent national character.

The syllabic writing consisting of 47 letters invented by Kūkai now came into practical use. We have already mentioned that the author, Kino Tsurayuki, used it for his prose works. Many writers followed his example, e.g. the unknown author of the Satire "Torikaebaya-monogatari,"[1] and the learned poetess Murasaki-Shikibu who lived at the imperial

---

[1] The story of the topsy-turvy world.

court, in her "Genji-monogatari,"[1] and the learned lady-in-waiting, Seishōnagon, in her regular reports of the events of the day destined for the court, which were collected under the title of "Makura-no-sōshi," and in her songs. At that time learned women and poetesses were no rarity at court. Girls received an excellent education. Women held as important a place at court as they did in European society. In the satire "Torikaebaya-monogatari" mentioned above, the unknown author scourges that condition of things and says, scoffingly, the men were women and the women men.

In architecture also, an independent spirit now ruled, and it was freed from Chinese influence. Beautiful gardens were laid out with fountains, ponds, and artificial eminences, and pretty country houses were built. Chinese costume went out of fashion, and clothes were made according to Japanese taste. The Japanese garment "Kimono," came into being. Japanese arts and industries developed independently, and furniture and utensils were made in their own taste. Painting and sculpture produced original talent. The painter Takuma Tamenari made his celebrated wall paintings at Uji in the royal temple Hōōdō, built by Uji-Kambaku, and Jōchō his well-known statues of Buddha.

When the tribe Joshin, which occupied a fairly independent position in Manchuria, attacked the inhabitants of the Japanese islands, Iki and Tsush-

---

[1] The story of the hero Genji.

MURASAKI-SHIKIBU

ima, Fujiwara Takaie, the President of the Dazaifu board which, as we have already said, governed the province of Tsukushi, successfully repulsed the enemy. But soon afterwards in the time of Go-Reizei-Tennō (1045-1068), the noble and great landed proprietor Abe-no-Yoritoki and his son set on foot a rebellion in the province of Mutsu. The Fujiwara were powerless against them, and the Emperor was compelled to beg help of the Minamoto against the rebels. After twelve years' fighting, the Minamoto succeeded in quelling the rising. During that time their military power increased, and they were soon strong enough in alliance with the Taira to put down the power of the hitherto ruling family of officials, the Fujiwara.

PART III

THE TAIRA AND MINAMOTO

CHAPTER X

ABOLITION OF GOVERNMENT BY GUARDIANS OF THE FUJIWARA FAMILY AND EMPERORS WHO HAD ABDICATED. GROWING POWER OF THE TAIRA AND MINAMOTO.

UNDER the guardianship of the Fujiwara family, the Emperor led a wretched sort of mock existence. They forced the adult Emperors to abdicate so that most of the Emperors who sat on the throne were minors. The imperial princes were married to daughters of the Fujiwara, and those alliances increased the power of the clan. But the Fujiwara, like the Emperors of an earlier time, gave themselves up to a life of luxury, wasted their strength in excesses, and entirely neglected to establish a military basis. So that directly a capable ruler came to the throne, he was able to free himself from their guardianship.

Such an Emperor was Go-Sanjō-Tennō (1068-1072). On his accession he directed all his efforts to put an end to the co-operation of the Fujiwara in the government and to restore the imperial family to power and esteem. As far as possible he ruled by himself, and the Fujiwara family and the rest of the nobility had to content themselves with administering their own property and the provinces they had gained. The Emperor forbade the officials to sell their posts and arranged that officials could only be appointed by himself. He practised great economy, and tried to curb the expenditure of the officials. And thus he was able somewhat to improve public order and administration. His last political idea was that the restoration of the guardianship of the Fujiwara must be prevented and that therefore the Emperor should abdicate in good time, and himself become the guardian of his successor. He put his idea into practice by abdicating himself, and continuing to govern as guardian. Then death overtook him.

His son, Shirakawa-Tennō (1072-1086), the 72nd Emperor, followed his father's example, and undertook the guardianship of his son, and after his death, of his grandson. And so the guardianship of the Fujiwara was abolished for ever. Yet they continued to hold a great position at court, since the most important offices of state were still filled by members of their family.

Shirakawa-Tennō did not inherit his father's economy. He built many temples, set up over 3,000 statues of Buddha, and undertook pilgrimages to the temples of Kōza and Kumano, both at a great distance from the capital. These pilgrimages cost large sums of money, since the Emperor was accompanied by a large and splendidly equipped suite. And so it came that he was forced to sell offices and privileges for money, and that in consequence the imperial power was weakened.

His piety and his submission to the Buddhist religion had a very bad result in the power of the priests who from that time became more and more overbearing. They even entered on wars, collected mercenary troops, and made private war. The temples of Enriakuji and Kōfukuji, especially, collected large armies and entered into bloody wars. They paid no heed to imperial decrees. In order to defy the government, they allied themselves more closely, made continual raids on Kiōto, and threatened the court there. Shirakawa-Tennō used to say: "As little as the weeds and the waters of the Kamogawa[1] obey my orders, as little do my priests heed them." The Taira and the Minamoto were his last refuge; he begged them to come to the capital to protect it from the attacks of the priests. A short time before, the Minamoto family had, at the Emperor's request, defeated Kiyowara Takehira, the imperial commander, and his nephew who had led an insurrection in the province of Mutsu. So the two military families became indispensable to the imperial court, and in time gained the same power as the Fujiwara had had before them.

[1] Kawa or Gawa = river.

CHAPTER XI

STRIFE IN THE IMPERIAL FAMILY. SUPREMACY OF THE TAIRA AND MINAMOTO

BLOODY dissensions that occurred in the imperial family itself contributed in an important degree to strengthen the power of the two ambitious military families.

After the death of Shirakawa-Tennō, his grandson, the Toba-Tennō who had abdicated, undertook the guardianship for his eldest son, Sutoku-Tennō (1123-1141). But he soon deposed him and set his youngest and favourite son, Konoe-Tennō (1141-1155), on the throne. He died, however, when he was sixteen years old, and then Toba-Tennō bestowed the imperial throne on another of his sons, Go-Shirakawa-Tennō (1155-1158). This roused the anger of his deposed eldest son, Sutoku-Tennō, who desired that he or his son should be Emperor. As long as his father lived, he controlled his anger, but on his death he assembled a large army, and laid siege to Go-Shirakawa-Tennō's palace. In sore need he was compelled to call in the help of Minamoto Yoshitomo and Taira Kiyomori, who after severe fighting put the deposed Sutoku-

Tennō to flight. He fell into the hands of the imperial army and was banished to the province of Sanuki in the island of Shikoku.

The two families, who in this manner acquired a most influential position at the imperial court, soon began to quarrel among themselves.

CHAPTER XII

HOSTILITY BETWEEN THE TAIRA AND MINAMOTO

MINAMOTO YOSHITOMO was a distinguished soldier, and Taira Kiyomori an astute statesman. The latter, through his friendship with Shinsai, an intriguing court official and a favourite of the Emperor, acquired greater influence and power at court than Minamoto. At that time also one of the Fujiwara named Nobuyori enjoyed the favour of Go-Shirakawa-Tennō. He sought by his intervention to get himself appointed general of the guards. But the Emperor at the instigation of Shinsai, the rival favourite, refused his request. Fujiwara sought a means of revenge and allied himself with Minamoto Yoshimoto who was an enemy of Taira Kiyomori, and his friend the courtier Shinsai. In 1159 Fujiwara and Minamoto came to open war with the Taira. They soon defeated them, occupied the imperial palace and for ten days ruled in the name of the Emperor. But the Taira quickly collected fresh troops with whom they now proceeded to gain a victory over their enemies. Fujiwara Nobuyori and Yoshitomo's eldest son were taken prisoners in the battle, and soon afterwards executed. Minamoto Yoshitomo fled, and hid among his vassals, but they, from fear of punishment, treacherously murdered him.

The Taira were now determined to render the Minamoto family harmless forever. They banished Yorimoto, the eldest of Yoshitomo's surviving sons (by his lawful wife) to the province of Izu where he was placed under the surveillance of Hōjō Tokimasa, one of their vassals. The other sons with their mother (a concubine of Yoshitomo) were taken prisoners in the country. The mother only saved her children's lives by giving herself to her deadly foe, Taira Kiyomori. The children, one of whom was later the famous Yoshitsune, were hidden in a monastery. The vassals of the conquered family were distributed through various districts of the land, and it seemed as if a restoration of the Minamoto was rendered absolutely impossible. But even in exile, their vassals remained loyal to them, and only waited until Yoshitomo's sons should be grown up, in order, under their leadership, to take up arms for their hereditary lords.

CHAPTER XIII

SUPREMACY AND FALL OF THE TAIRA

AFTER this war the Taira held all the power in their own hands. Kiyomori was chancellor-in-chief and received the title of Juichii.[1] His daughter was the wife of Takakura-Tennō (1168-1180). His sons and other relatives, sixteen in number, were ministers, or held other high offices. Half of the whole of the Japanese Empire was in the private ownership of the Taira family. It was said at that time that no one who did not belong to the race of the Taira was a man. The family soon became so arrogant and proud that it was universally hated.

Even Go-Shirakawa-Tennō who had abdicated, had to suffer under their authority and tried to free himself from it. Therefore his favourite Fujiwara Narichika brought together many malcontents in the house of the priest Shunkan in the village of Shishi-ga-dani, and they formed a conspiracy. They were discovered, and the conspirators were put to death or exiled. Taira Kiyomori conceived a plan

[1] The highest title that an official can hold in his lifetime.

Taira Shigemori

SUPREMACY AND FALL OF THE TAIRA 79

to imprison Go-Shirakawa-Tennō, whom he entirely mistrusted. But his son, Shigemori, who remained loyal to the deposed Emperor was able for some time to prevent its execution. When, however, he had died of grief for his father's many misdeeds, the latter kept Go-Shirakawa-Tennō a prisoner in a castle near the capital.

But when soon after the wife of the Emperor Takakura, the daughter of Taira Kiyomori, bore a son, Kiyomori compelled Takakura-Tennō to abdicate, and placed the new-born infant on the throne as Antoku-Tennō (1180-1185) in order to assume the guardianship for his grandson. He now felt himself secure in power, and kept a brilliant and luxurious court. And his officials and all the members of his family did likewise and led a life of luxury and dissipation, in absolute certainty of the strength of their supremacy.

But the Minamoto and their dependents had never ceased to plan an attack on their enemies.

Minamoto Yoshitsune left the monastery, and fled to the north of the empire, where he prepared himself for the coming fight by many a knightly adventure. Meanwhile Minamoto Yoritomo had made friends with his guardian, Hōjō Tokimasa, and had married his daughter. He was the real leader of the conspiracy against the Taira. Secretly the Minamoto won adherents and economised their strength. It was of the greatest importance that the son of the imprisoned Go-Shirakawa-Tennō should support them, and with his consent, Minamoto Yoritomo began to collect troops in the province of Izu, while his cousin, Minamoto

Yoshinaka, collected the sinews of war in the province of Shinano.

Taira Kiyomori was not to live to see the end of the struggle. On hearing of the rebellion he sent a powerful army against Yoritomo, but it could do nothing against him, and after receiving the news of the defeat Kiyomori died.

Minamoto Yoshinaka had meanwhile succeeded in subduing the province of Shinano, and soon conquered also the territory lying to the north-west of the province. He put an army sent against him by the Taira to flight, and pursued it even to the capital. The Taira then fled with the young Antoku-Tennō and the insignia[1] preserved in the imperial palace, to the west of Japan.

Go-Shirakawa-Tennō returned to the capital from his prison. He set up Go-Toba-Tennō, a half-brother of Antoku-Tennō as Emperor, so that there were now two Emperors.

Strife soon broke out between the victors. By his insolent and cruel government Minamoto Yoshinaka evoked the hostility of Go-Shirakawa, the guardian of

---

[1] The insignia consisted of copies of the mirror and sword. According to the Nihongi, Sujin-Tennō built a temple in Kasanui (province of Yamato) for the mirror and sword that had been presented by Amaterasu-Omikami. At the same time he had copies made of them which were preserved in the imperial palace together with the Magatama. Under Suinin-Tennō the real mirror and sword were kept in another place. He built a new temple for them in the province of Ise on the Isuzu where they continued to be preserved.

BATTLE OF THE MINAMOTO AND TAIRA

SUPREMACY AND FALL OF THE TAIRA 81

the Emperor. He summoned Minamoto Yoritomo to his aid, who meanwhile had made Kamakura in the plain of Kantō his residence and from there directed the enterprise against the Taira. Yoritomo sent an army against Yoshinaka under the command of his brothers of whom Yoshitsune especially distinguished himself by deeds of valour. They were victorious and by the order of Yoritomo they put Yoshinaka to death.

The Taira thought to use these quarrels of the Minamoto family to regain their old supremacy. They ventured an attack on the capital which was an entire failure. Driven back they fled into the province of Sanuki. The Minamoto pursued them, and gained a victory over them, and the Taira had to take refuge in their ships and flee to the west. But there, too, they were pursued by land or sea by their victorious adversaries. When they tried to land on the coast of the Dan-no-ura Sea it was already occupied by the Minamoto. Some who tried to effect a landing by force, fell in the struggle, and the rest were drowned. The Emperor's grandmother, the widow of Taira Kiyomori, threw herself into the sea with the young Antoku-Tennō and the imperial insignia. And so after a supremacy of thirty years the Taira family was destroyed for ever (1185).

The imperial family for whom the Taira had become too powerful did not long enjoy the triumph of their downfall. They had had a dangerous ally in the struggle, one who was now all powerful and able to secure greater authority in the Empire than the Taira had possessed.

THIRD PERIOD

FROM THE FOUNDATION OF THE KAMAKURA SHOGUNATE TO THE END OF THE TOKUGAWA SHOGUNATE (FEUDAL PERIOD)

PART I

THE KAMAKURA SHOGUNATE

CHAPTER I.

FOUNDATION OF THE KAMAKURA SHOGUNATE BY THE MINAMOTO FAMILY. THEIR SUPREMACY AND THEIR FALL THROUGH THE HOJO FAMILY

IT has been already stated that Minamoto Yoritomo, at the time of the downfall of his family, had taken up his residence at Kamakura in the eastern province of Sagami, and thence conducted the military enterprises of his family. The Samurai-dokoro, the officials appointed by Yoritomo for military affairs, had their seat there. When the whole power came into the hands of the Minamoto, Kamakura became the real seat of government. Yoritomo appointed Kumonjo or Mandokoro, the actual government officials, with Monjusho to be officers of justice. The councils appointed by Yoritomo at Kamakura possessed in reality the power of the government. The old Dajōkan and the ministers and councils working under him, remained in the imperial capital Kiōto, but their offices were merely titular. They no longer possessed real practical power. In 1192 Go-Toba Tennō sent an embassy to Yoritomo which appointed him Shogun, i.e. commander-in-chief. Thence comes the term,

Shōgunate of Kamakura. As Shōgun, Yoritomo was the sole head of the government. He levied taxes, and was especially careful to collect those due for the army, and paid his soldiers. He rewarded those who had been loyal to him with large grants of land. He was respectful to the Emperor and formally recognised him as the actual ruler. In reality the sovereign did not possess the slightest power in the country, and exercised no influence on Yoritomo's government.

The foundation of the Shōgunate was not a mere chance or passing event in the historical development of Japan nor must it be regarded merely as the act of any one great man like Yoritomo. It was the result of a long evolution which marks the essential character of the Japanese Empire, the evolution of the feudal system which had its beginnings in the time of the Fujiwara. Yoritomo owed the power to acquire so independent a position with regard to the Emperor and the government of the state entirely to the loyalty of his vassals who, during the period of persecution, had remained faithful to him, and the powerful position of great families like the Taira and Minamoto was only a circumstance in the evolution of the feudal system. In the course of the last centuries new powers had arisen. The power of the Emperor and of the imperial officials was wholly abolished by the power of the feudal lords, the Daimiōs, who relied on the support of their vassals, the Samurai, whom we may already call knights. The actual reins of government were held by the most powerful of the feudal lords, the Shōgun.

MINAMOTO YORITOMO

THE KAMAKURA-SHOGUNATE

With the establishment of the Shōgunate a new epoch of Japanese history began, just as the great reforms of the Taika years formed another. With some breaks, the Shōgunate remained the prevailing form of government until quite modern times, until Japan came into closer relations with Europe.

Simultaneously with the progress and change due to the feudal system in the political conditions of Japan, there were also important ethical developments in the Japanese nation which the Japanese call "Bushidō" (chivalry). Bushidō is of fundamental importance for the moral outlook of the Japanese nation, and we shall often have to speak of it in greater detail.

Yoritomo understood how to use the new development for his own aims. He possessed great organizing and administrative talent, and succeeded in founding a new central government and bringing the whole of the empire under its sway. But side by side with his great intellectual gifts and his energy, he had serious faults of character. Only too soon he showed himself accessible to the evil influence of the Hōjō family to which he owed his life, and from among whom he had chosen a wife. Through them he persecuted his brave brother, Yoshitsune, who had gained many laurels in the late fighting and who together with his friend Benkei is still celebrated in the songs of the poets. When Yoshitsune saw that his brother had designs on his life, he fled, and raised a rebellion which was unsuccessful. Finally he was murdered by a great noble in Mutsu. Yoritomo also got rid of his younger brother Noriyori, and so through his own fault the supremacy of his family was soon ended by the very persons in whom he had put his trust.

On the death of Yoritomo, his son Yoriie became Shōgun. After four years his grandfather, Hōjō Tokimasa, banished him, and then had him murdered. His brother Sanetomo, the third Shōgun, succumbed to a plot of Hōjō Yoshitoki, the son of Tokimasa. He was the last of Yoritomo's descendants. But the ruin of the Minamoto family, through the establishment of the Shōgunate had little influence on the new political ordering of the state.

CHAPTER II

ESTABLISHMENT OF THE SUPREMACY OF THE HOJO FAMILY. *FAINEANTS* SHOGUNS AND SHIKKEN.

WHEN the Minamoto family became extinct with the murder of the third Shōgun by Hōjō Yoshitoki, the Hōjō family could not at once gain possession of the Shōgunate, as they were not of noble birth. They had originally not been freemen, and had only won respect in military service with great nobles, at last with the Taira. None of the great families of the nobility would have recognised a Hōjō as Shōgun. Therefore Hōjō Yoshitoki first summoned a one year old boy of the Fujiwara from the capital, appointed him Shōgun, and conducted the government for him under the title of Shikken, i.e. deputy of the commander-in-chief.

Go-Toba-Tennō, the deposed Emperor, disliked the tyrannical rule of the Shikken, and decided to crush the Hōjō family by means of his son, Juntoku-Tennō. For that purpose Juntoku-Tennō abdicated, and his son Chūkiō-Tennō ascended the throne.

The preparations made by the imperial family were betrayed to Hōjō Yoshitoki. He immediately sent his brother and his son with an army against the capital. A battle with the troops which the Emperor hurriedly collected ensued and resulted in their defeat. Yoshitoki deposed Chūkiō-Tennō, raised his cousin Go-Horikawa-Tennō to the throne, and sent Go-Toba-Tennō, the instigator of the rebellion, and his family, into exile. He placed a permanent garrison in the capital under the command of a Rokuhara-Tandai, who had surveillance over the Emperor, and had the right of deciding whether an emperor should remain on the throne or should abdicate.

Hōjō Yasutoki, son of Yoshitoki, and also his son, Tokiyori, had prosperous and happy reigns. Yasutoki instituted a law comprising 51 articles relating to the new order of knights. It was called Jōei-Shikimoku [1] after the Jōei year (1232) in which it was proclaimed. Tokiyori made an imperial prince Shōgun, and the innovation had the result that for the future the Shōgunate was always held by princes, generally minors.

---

[1] Shikimoku = law.

Mongolian Ship Attacked by Japanese

CHAPTER III

REPULSE OF MONGOLIAN ATTEMPTS AT INVASION

THE most important event in the reign of the Shikken is the repulse of the Mongolian attacks on Japan.

Mangkan, king of the Mongols, grandson of the famous Dshingiskhan who had pillaged eastern Europe from 1219 to 1225, and cousin of the Bathu who conquered Russia, and penetrated victoriously as far as Liegnitz in Silesia (1241), ordered his brother Khubilai-khan to bring China under his sway. Khubilai-khan succeeded in subduing a large part of China and Korea. When by the death of his brother, he became lord of Mongolia and the conquered territories, he made Peking his capital, and sent ambassadors to Japan to demand that the Emperor should recognise his supremacy. But at the instigation of the Shikken the embassy was sent back. Khubilai-khan equipped a fleet which with 30,000 men sailed the sea to conquer the Japanese islands. Hōjō Tokimune prevented them from landing, and on their return the whole fleet was destroyed by a storm. In order to protect himself from further attacks, Hōjō Tokimune fortified the bay of Hakata, which was the chief place where the enemy would land, and put a strong garrison there.

In 1281, in the reign of Go-Uda-Tennō (1274-1287), Kubilai-khan again sent a large fleet with an army 100,000 men strong to Japan, but the cleverness of Hōjō Tokimune and the courage of the Japanese warriors enabled them to repel the attack and the hostile fleet was again destroyed by a storm on their return voyage. Only a few of the Mongols were saved and returned home. That was the last time that a foreign foe attempted to conquer Japan.

The war, however, for the first time, gave opportunity to a European, the Venetian traveller, Marco Polo, who was then living at the Court of Kubilai-khan, to learn something about Japan, and he published the result of his studies in his travels as an account of Jipang.

CHAPTER IV

ART, LEARNING AND RELIGION AT THE TIME OF THE KAMAKURA-SHOGUNATE.

THE disturbances during the time of the Taira and Minamoto had not destroyed the beginnings made in art and learning during the Nara and Fujiwara time. They found no place, however, among the knightly order. The knights cared only for fighting, and spent times of peace in military exercises, tournaments, wrestling, shooting with the bow, etc. If the young Samurai learnt to read, he confined his reading to tales of the heroic deeds of his ancestors.

But a very different life prevailed at the imperial court. Shut out entirely from political and military activities, there was leisure for the encouragement of learning and especially of poetry. Japan reckons as its best poets, Go-Toba-Tennō, Juntoko-Tennō, Fujiwara Shūnzei and his son Fujiwara Teika, Fujiwara Ietaka and the Buddhist priest, Saigiō.

The Buddhist priests had great importance in the development of Japanese culture. For Buddhism had just entered on a new epoch. Hitherto that religion had, on account of its philosophical character, been confined to the educated class, for it was too difficult for the unlearned to understand. Buddhism was first made accessible to the common people, through the sects which practiced a wide tolerance, took heed of the needs of the people, and understood how to make their teaching comprehended by all. They have already been mentioned as the Tendai-Shū and Shingon-Shū. The following are the most important of the later sects. The priest, Hōnen-Shōnin, founded the Jōdō-shū.[1] The chief doctrine of that sect was that salvation could only be obtained by the grace of Buddha and that men must unceasingly pray: "Namu amida butsu," i.e. "I trust in Buddha." Shinran-Shōnin, the pupil of Hōnen-Shōnin, founded the Shin-shū. That sect permitted marriage and the eating of meat. Nichiren-Shōnin founded a sect which bore the name Nichiren-Shū after him, or Hokke-Shū after his teaching. Contrary to the "Namu amida butsu," of the Jōdō-Shū, he taught the prayer: "Namu miō hōren gekiō," i.e. "I trust in the beautiful Hokekiō." Hokekiō is according to Nichiren the classic book of Buddha's doctrine.

Through these sects Buddhism not only became extremely powerful in Japan and the prevailing religion, but it led also to the secular progress of the land. Buddhist priests occupied themselves more than formerly with secular tasks, poetry, the arts and learning. Saigiō, for example, was a famous poet.

[1] Jōdo = the kingdom of God. Shū = sect.

Art-loving Buddhist priests encouraged the painters, Tosa Mitsunaga and Fujiwara Nobuzane, and the carvers, Unkei and Tankei to produce their famous works which were mostly destined to adorn Buddhist temples.

The manufacture of pottery, especially, made progress among the people.

CHAPTER V

DIVISION OF THE IMPERIAL LINE. ABOLITION OF THE SHOGUNATE

GO-SAGA-TENNO (1242-1246) preferred his younger son to the elder who had already ascended the throne as Go-Fukakusa-Tennō (1246-1259); he compelled Go-Fukakusa-Tennō to abdicate, and the younger son became Emperor with the name Kameyana-Tennō (1259-1274). And Go-Saga-Tennō determined that the Imperial dignity should remain for ever in the Kameyana family. Therefore Go-Fukakusa-Tennō allied himself with the Shikken, Hōjō Tokimune, and with his aid, after the death of Go-Saga-Tennō, placed his son on the throne as Fushimi-Tennō (1287-1298), and deposed his younger brother. Sadatoki, son of Hōjō Tokimune, at first attached himself to the line of the elder brother, and placed the son of Fushimi-Tennō on the throne as Go-Fushimi-Tennō (1298-1301). But in consequence of the continual complaints of Go-Uda-Tennō (1274-1287), who had abdicated, about the violation of his grandfather's will, he determined later that in future each line should reign alternately. The chief branch of the elder brother,

Go-Fukakusa-Tennō, was henceforth called Ji-miō-in, for after his abdication he lived at Ji-miō-in; the chief branch of the younger was called Daigagu-ji after the temple of Daigagu-ji which it had made its seat.

The Shikken, Hōjō Takatoki, the son of Sadatoki, led a dissipated and extravagant life and practised great cruelties. And so all the people hated him, and desired that he should be removed. The reigning Emperor, Go-Daigo-Tennō (1318-1339), who belonged to the Daigagu-ji branch, thought the opportunity had come to free himself from the Shikken's authority, and to put an end to the Shōgunate for ever. But his plan became known to the Shikken who in 1331 sent a large army against the capital. The imperial army succumbed. The Emperor was taken prisoner as he fled, and banished to the island of Oki. The Shikken chose the new Emperor, Kōgon-Tennō, from the other branch.

The war roused public opinion, and a strong imperial party came into being, the object of which was the fall of the Shikken. As adherents of the Emperor may be mentioned: Kusunoki Masashige, Akamatsu Norimura, Nawa Nagatoshi, and the Nitta and Ashikaga families who were both descended from the Minamoto family. Nitta Yoshisada collected troops in his province of Kōzuke and marched to Kamakura. During the siege, Hōjō Takatoki and his whole family and his adherents took refuge in a temple where they all, about 200 in number, committed suicide. Meanwhile Go-Daigo-Tennō had returned from the island of Oki. Nawa Nagatoshi had assembled troops for him in the province of Hōki, and with them he began to conquer the neighbouring provinces. Kusunoki Masashige led a rebellion in support of Go-Daigo-Tennō in the province of Kawachi which was situated near the capital. Ashikagu Takauji, another adherent of Go-Daigo-Tennō, a few weeks after the fall of the Hōjō family, succeeded in taking possession of the capital. After Go-Daigo-Tennō and his supporters had marched into the capital, Kōgon-Tennō who owed his crown to Hōjō-Takatoki, abdicated, and left the throne to Go-Daigo-Tennō who was now actually in sole possession of the government (1333).

But the Emperor only enjoyed for a brief space the independence of which for the last 150 years, the throne had been deprived by the Shōgunate.

PART II

RESTORATION, DIVISION, AND RECONCILIATION
OF THE IMPERIAL DYNASTY

CHAPTER VI

REIGN AND FALL OF GO-DAIGO-TENNO

AFTER his entry into the capital, Go-Daigo-Tennō ruled the whole Empire himself. He gave the command of the army to Prince Morinaga, appointed Prince Norinaga, governor of the north, and Prince Narinaga, who had hitherto been Shōgun in Kamakura, governor of the city and of the plain of Kantō. The position of the old imperial officials like the Dajōkan, and his subordinate ministers who under the Shōgunate had sunk into entire insignificance, was now improved although they never regained their former importance, as the Emperor appointed new officials and gave them the actual power. These changes in the government were known as the reforms of the Kemmu year.

Only a portion of the men who had distinguished themselves in the war received great rewards. Many went unrewarded, while many court favourites received gifts beyond their deserts. Complaints soon arose in the army about the conferring of distinctions. The ill-feeling increased the more it was recognised that under the imperial government the military element lost the importance it had had under the Shōgunate, and the more the imperial civil officials and the courtiers triumphed over it.

The people, too, were infected by the discontent, for in spite of the heavy taxes which oppressed them as a result of the war, the Emperor built new palaces and kept an extravagant court. Nearly everyone began to long for the former government.

Ashikaga Takauji desired to make use of the discontent to restore the Shōgunate government in favour of his family. Prince Morinaga was clever enough to scent out the plan, told the Emperor of his fears, and tried to make it of no avail. But Ashikaga slandered him to the Emperor, and effected his banishment to Kamakura where he had him murdered.

When Hōjō Tokiyuki, the only Hōjō who at the destruction of the family was saved by a servant, raised a rebellion in Kamakura, he seized the opportunity to obtain the command of the army from the Emperor with the order to suppress the rebels. He increased his army by recruiting a large number of malcontents who were ready to rebel against the imperial rule. After defeating Hōjō, he publicly put himself in opposition to the Emperor.

The Emperor ordered Nitta Yoshisada to subdue him. But after several battles in the mountains of Hakone, Nitta's army was destroyed, and Nitta himself fled with what remained of it to Kiōtō. Then Akamatsu Norimura who was also dissatisfied with the Imperial government went over to Ashikaga with a large body of troops, and they took the capital. Go-Daigo-Tennō fled to the temple on the hill of Hiei. Meanwhile Nitta Yoshisada had assembled a fresh band of combatants among the Emperor's adherents, and hurried secretly with them to the capital, attacked Ashikaga's army, put it to flight, and recaptured the town for the Emperor who was able to return again, but only for a short time.

Ashikaga fled to the island of Kiūsū and began there, supported by the authority of Kōgon-Tennō (of the other imperial branch), to collect fresh troops in order to march again on the capital. His friend Akamatsu attacked the imperial troops led by Nitta Yoshisada, which had pursued Ashikaga to Kiūsiū, and were here entirely destroyed, and kept them fighting until Ashikaga had collected his new army, and made an attack on the imperial capital. When Nitta received the news of Ashikaga's march on Kiōtō, he took up an advantageous position near the village of Hiōgo, and there awaited the hostile army. Ashikaga now joined with Akamatsu, and soon after, near Hiōgo, with his brother who had hastened from Kiūsiū with a fleet. A fierce battle took place at Hiōgo in which the imperial army was defeated. The imperial commander, Kusunoki Masashige, killed himself during the fight. Nitta Yoshisada fled back into the capital which was soon besieged by the enemy. Go-Daigo-Tennō again took refuge in the temple on the hill of Hiei, and Nitta Yoshisada escaped to the north with the crown prince and the other princes. Ashikaga took possession of the capital, and placed a prince of the other imperial line, Kōmiō-Tennō[1] on the throne (1336).

[1] He was a brother of Kōgon-Tennō.

CHAPTER VII

DYNASTIES OF THE NORTH AND SOUTH

FROM the temple on the hill of Hiei, Go-Daigo-Tennō fled to the province of Yamato, south of the capital, and lived there in the village of Yoshino. There were again two Emperors in Japan, a dynasty of the north and a dynasty of the south. The imperial insignia was in possession of the dynasty of the south, and it was therefore regarded as the rightful imperial line. If its dominions only included a small part of the empire, it possessed much sympathy in the land of the opposing dynasty, and numbered the best men of the Empire among its adherents. The division lasted for 56 years and during that time, three Emperors of the southern, and five of the northern dynasty reigned. The whole period was one of fighting between the two families, and actual war prevailed for 20 years without a break.

In 1349, Ashikaga, who then possessed the real governing power in the Empire of the northern dynasty, commanded his general, Kōno Moronao, to march with the whole army against the southern dynasty. Kusunoki Masatsura (son of the Kusunoki

Masashige who had committed suicide at the decisive defeat of the rightful Emperor), who like his father remained faithful to his imperial house, marched out with all his adherents to attack him in the field of Shijōnawate. A battle ensued in which despite their courage the adherents of the rightful line were defeated. Kusunoki Masatsura and his whole family committed suicide. Kōno Moronao attacked the imperial palace, and Go-Murakami-Tennō, son of Go-Daigo-Tennō had to flee farther to the south. His former palace was razed to the ground. Tennō was not pursued farther, for the valley in which he had taken refuge was surrounded by mountains, the passes of which could be easily defended, and so Go-Murakami-Tennō made Kanō in that district his place of residence.

But soon the victorious northern dynasty was weakened by the numerous rebellions in their kingdom. All the Daimiōs who were striving for independence used these divisions in the reigning family to gain their independence. They left the northern dynasty under the pretext that they only dared to obey the rightful Emperor, and supported by their Samurai vassals, they attained absolute independence. There were innumerable struggles between the different Daimiōs since each sought to extend his possessions, and universal anarchy prevailed in the land. Those disturbances were the harbingers of the later hundred years' war.

Amid the confusion, Ashikaga Takauji obtained the consent of the northern dynasty to the restoration of the Shōgunate. Following the example of the former Shōgunate of Kamakura, he placed new Shōgunate councils at Kiōto. It was hoped that the councils which differed from the imperial civil service through their military authority, would be able to restore order.

The Shōgun, Ashikaga Takauji and his son who succeeded him in the office, again took up the struggle against the southern dynasty. But as it was impossible to carry on the war, and at the same time to introduce improvements into the domestic affairs of the Empire, the third Shōgun Yoshimitsu (1368-1394) thought it wiser to make peace with the southern dynasty. In 1392 an embassy of the Shōgun conducted Go-Kameyama-Tennō, the Emperor of the southern dynasty to Kiōto where a reconciliation between him and Go-Komatsu-Tennō, the Emperor of the northern dynasty, took place. Go-Kameyama-Tennō abdicated, and delivered over the imperial insignia to Go-Komatsu-Tennō. Therefore he recognized him as father, and the whole Empire was again united under one dynasty.

PART III

THE MUROMACHI OR ASHIKAGA SHOGUNATE

CHAPTER VIII

THE MUROMACHI SHOGUNATE

AT first the new Shōguns had a very difficult position. They were very far from actually governing the whole Empire. The numerous rebellions of the nobles in the land stood in the way, as well as the pride and arrogance of those who were second in command whom they were obliged to pay very highly for their services, and who, notwithstanding, often refused to carry out their orders. Yoshimitsu, the third Shōgun, was the first who made his influence felt throughout the land after the peace with the southern dynasty left him free to deal with internal disorders. He found strong support in Hosokawa Yoriyuki, one of the great nobles. With his help he put down the powerful family, Yamana Ujikiyo, who owned the sixth part of the whole empire.

After Yoshimitsu had made the Shōgunate fairly universally recognised in the Empire, he erected in a street of Kiōto, Muromachi, new and splendid government offices for the Shōgunate, which for that reason was from that time known as the "Shōgunate of Muramachi." The chief official under the Shōgun was the Kanriō, who although he possessed great power, did not gain so important a position as the Shikken had formerly had, for three rival families laid claim to the office of Kanriō. These families were the Shiba, Hosokawa and Hatakeyama, and they were known as the three Kanriō families. The rest of the officials were the same as those of the Shōgunate of Kamakura.

The district of Kamakura had now a certain importance of its own, for the first Shōgun had established there a subordinate government for the family of his second son. The heads of that government were called Kamakura-Kanriō or Kantō-Kanriō.

Yoshimitsu provided for the fortification of the frontiers on the north and south. Instead of the usual governors he appointed Tandai in the frontier provinces who possessed special military authority. The administration of the other provinces lay, as under the Shōgunate of Kamakura, in the hands of Shugo.

When Yoshimitsū became old, he abdicated, and was succeeded by his son, Yoshimochi. Yoshimitsu built himself a magnificent palace in the neighbourhood of the capital on the Kitayama,[1] called Kinkaku, (i.e. golden, many-storied building). As "Lord of Kitayama" he lived in great splendour, and as was the custom of the Emperor after his abdication, never showed himself in public unless accompanied by a brilliant train of followers. He treated the imperial court officials as his servants. The Shōgun also

[1] Kita=north : Yama=hill.

adopted a similar luxurious way of living, and it resulted that the Shōgun families, like the Fujiwara family of an earlier date, degenerated through luxury and dissipation so that the administration of government and the real power passed into the hands of the Kanriō.

CHAPTER IX

THE DISORDERS OF THE ONIN YEARS AND THE STRUGGLE FOR THE SUPREMACY OF KAMAKURA

THE eighth Shōgun, Yoshimasa (1449-1472), led a profligate and extravagant life, and cared little about administering the state. The disorder that resulted in the Empire encouraged the ambitious and powerful general, Yamana Sōzen, to attempt to gain a more important position for himself. With the concurrence of the Shōgun, he began war on the wealthy and powerful family, Akamatsu, in 1441; he defeated them and enriched himself with their possessions. After this good fortune he ventured to oppose the Kanriō Hosokawa Katsumoto. He managed to make himself agreeable to the Shōgun's wife so that he was appointed guardian of her son who was a minor, and endeavoured to make him the future Shōgun, although Shōgun Yoshimasa had expressly determined that his own brother whose guardian was the Kanriō, Hosokawa Katsumoto, should be the next Shōgun. The cause which was to turn the strained relations between Yamana Sōzen and Hosokawa Katsumoto into open war was not long in arising.

DISORDERS OF THE ONIN YEARS

At the same time a bitter quarrel raged between the members of the Kanriō family, Shiba, and the members of the Kanriō family, Hatakeyama, as to which of the families was to be the future Kanriō. In 1467, the first of the Onin years, it came to open war with the Hatakeyama family. When the Kanriō interfered in the struggle and declared himself on the side of one of the rival parties, Yamana Sōzen put himself and all his power on the side of the other. Then the two parties of the Shiba family joined in the strife, one taking the side of the Kanriō, the other of Yamana Sōzen. And so the whole army and the whole land were involved in a civil war which lasted ten years.

During the struggle, the capital was repeatedly set on fire. The fine temples and palaces were destroyed, and with them magnificent works of art and valuable manuscripts. The two generals, Kanriō and Yamana Sōzen, died in the course of the war, which only ended because the strength of both sides was utterly exhausted.

A still bloodier civil war raged in the district of Kamakura.

The Kamakura Kanriō had, as time went on, become more powerful and arrogant. He claimed the same honours as those enjoyed by the Shōgun. Mochiuji, the greatgrandson of the first Kantō Kanriō, resisted the orders of the Shōgunate, and made a plan to throw off the supremacy of the capital, Kiōto. When Uesugi Norizane, one of his nobles, warned him of the danger of such an attempt, he threatened him with death. Uesugi Norizane then revealed the plot of the insurrection to the Shōgun. The Shōgun sent a large army against Mochiuji which he was unable to withstand. He was defeated in the first battle and then committed suicide (1439).

The Onin war now followed, into which Kamakura and its district was also drawn.

After a long struggle, Uesugi Noritada, the son of Norizane, although he had himself held the office of a Kantō Kanriō, and had won some power for his family during the disorders, finally appointed Shigeuji, the son of Mochiuji, as Kantō Kanriō. But he cherished a distrust of his benefactor who had been responsible for his father's fall, and had him murdered, a deed which resulted in fresh violent struggles. The Uesugi family summoned their vassals and adherents against Shigeuji. He could not withstand their attacks; he fled to the province of Shimōsa and lived there at Koga where he built himself a small palace. He was thenceforth called Koga Kubō. The Uesugi family now appointed Masatomo, brother of the 8th Shōgun, Yoshimasa, Kantō Kanriō, so that there were two rulers. The situation was made more complicated through the quarrel which broke out in the Uesugi family itself. It divided into two parties which fought against each other. One of them which was hostile to the new Kantō Kanriō, besieged the capital, Kamakura, and prevented the Kanriō from taking up his residence there. He therefore set up his dwelling place at Horigoe in the province of Izu, and was thenceforth called Horigoe Kubō. After a while he was murdered there by his eldest son, because he preferred his younger son.

These disorders only ended when a distinguished man, Ise Naganji, (or Hōjō Sōun) came to the province of Izu. He defeated Masatomo's undutiful son and conquered the province of Izu and its neighbourhood, and as we shall see later, his family gained all the districts belonging to Kamakura.

CHAPTER X

THE AGE OF HIGASHIYAMA.[1] ART, LITERATURE, AND LEARNING

YOSHIMASA, the 8th Shōgun, abdicated in order to give himself up to the extravagant life of pleasure, which he preferred to the serious business of government. He took up his residence in Higashiyama, in the eastern quarter of the capital, Kiōto, where he kept a court of great magnificence, the brilliance of which was long remembered in the whole empire, and gave a name to the period. Yoshimasa built there a two-storied palace called Ginkaku.[2] He adorned the interior with manuscripts of songs artistically written, paintings and other objects of art, and there, among other things, the ceremonial tea-drinking took place. The extravagance of the court put a great strain on the financial resources of the country, and increased the people's burden of taxation. But nevertheless, the Ashikaga, despite their extravagant leanings, had their merits. They were warm patrons of the revival of the arts that

[1] Higashi=east, Yama=hill or mountain.
[2] i.e. the silver, several storied building.

THE AGE OF HIGASHIYAMA

took place at this time, strengthened the relations with China again, and in so doing especially considered the financial advantages to themselves.

Among the famous painters of this period, Sesshū, Kanō-Masanobu, and his son Monotobu, deserve mention. Monotobu was the founder of a school of which the aim was to make a compromise between Chinese and Japanese painting.

Chinese porcelain was also again introduced into Japan at this time; since its former alliance with Japan, China had made great progress in that branch of manufacture. Artistic smith's work also flourished then in Japan; a well-known artist of that kind was Gotō Yūjō.

A new epoch began in architecture, for houses were built without windows. They had wooden outer walls, the panels of which could be removed, and were only fixed in at night; but in the day-time doors were arranged made of paper resembling glass which let in air and light.

Among the poets of the period, the song writers Fujiwara Kanera and Ota Dōkan must be named. Ota Dōkan is one of the few poets of the order of chivalry.

Learning was confined almost entirely to the Buddhist priests; outside their ranks only the library of Kanazawa and the school of Ashikaga had any importance.

CHAPTER XI

THE HEROIC AGE (1478-1573)

THE settlement of the war of the Onin years and of the struggle for the supremacy of Kamakura, brought Japan no lasting peace. On the contrary, those struggles only formed the prelude to the bloody "Hundred Years' War." For the space of a hundred years, every part of the empire was torn by various struggles and feuds. It was a time when individual ability alone decided the issue. He who yesterday was merely one of the retinue of a great man, was to-day himself the ruler. It was the heroic age of Japan, a time of great deeds of brave knights. Four Emperors reigned during the hundred years' war: Go-Tsuchimikado-Tennō (1464-1500); Go-Kashiwahara-Tennō (1500-1526); Go-Nara-Tennō (1526-1557); and Ogimachi-Tennō (1557-1587). During the period the families of the military nobility that had had the upper hand were almost annihilated, especially the Ashikaga family which had formerly been in possession of the Shōgunate.

Let us now consider the fate of the central power during these struggles.

THE HEROIC AGE

The Shōgun, Ashikaga Yoshitane, was banished by his Kanriō Hosokawa Masamoto. When a quarrel arose in the Hosokawa family, Ouchi Yoshioki, a great noble, who had remained faithful to the Shōgun, succeeded in bringing him back to the capital, and in deposing the Shōgun, Yoshigumi, set up by the Hosokawa family. Ashikaga Yoshitane remained in possession of the Shōgunate for thirteen years while Ouchi Yoshioki occupied a position in regard to him similar to that held formerly by the Shōgun to the Emperor.

When after ten years Ouchi Yoshioki retired from office and returned home, the Hosokawa family again came into prominence; it appropriated the office of a Kanriō and deposed the Shōgun, Ashikaga Yoshitane. His nephew, Ashikaga Yoshiharu, was now appointed 12th Shōgun. Under his reign strife once more broke out in the Hosokawa Kanriō family. Miyoshi Chōkei, one of their vassals, attained great power during the strife, and became the real leader of the Kanriō office, and was in regard to the Kanriō, as the Kanriō to the Shōgun and the Shōgun to the Emperor. Miyoshi Chōkei was even able to depose the Shōgun, and make his son, Yoshiteru, Shōgun.

After the death of Miyoshi Chōkei. his vassal, Matsunaga Hisahide, came into possession of the real power, so that the noble families were dependent on their subordinates. Finally Matsunaga Hisahide murdered the Shōgun, Ashikaga Yoshiteru, and appointed his cousin, Ashikaga Yoshihide, Shōgun.

After his death Ashikaga Yoshiaki was appointed

Shōgun by Oda Nobunaga, a knight who had attained power through the struggles of the time. The Shōgun tried to acquire independence, and to free himself from the guardianship of Oda Nobunaga. But Oda Nobunaga who held the actual power, deposed him, and sent him into exile. And therewith ended the Shōgunate of the Ashikaga family (1573). For the next thirty years there was as a rule no Shōgunate.

Nevertheless, the imperial family remained in their old insignificant position. It had suffered as greatly as the Shōgunate in the disorders. Already in the struggles of the Onin years the central government had not been able to ensure the regular collection of the taxes, and the Emperor fell into serious financial difficulties. The imperial palace was not kept in proper repair, the walls fell down, and the place that had hitherto been concealed from the sight of the people like a sanctuary, became accessible to all. As there was no longer feasting at court, the courtiers and high dignitaries wandered through the land and sought employment and shelter with the great nobles. When Go-Tsuchimikado-Tennō died, his family had not money enough to bury him, and were obliged to borrow the necessary funds from the military territorial nobility. His son, Go-Kashiwahara-Tennō, could only defray the cost of the ceremonies connected with his accession by money supplied by the Buddhist priests. His son, Go-Nara Tennō, likewise, could only celebrate his accession by means of borrowed money. In order to provide for his support, he had to write songs for pay. As the purchasers might not look on the Emperor who was naturally worshipped as a descendant of the gods, they put the money with the commission behind a curtain of the palace, and after a while fetched the manuscript away.

The real power of the government was not in the capital, but in the country with the heroic Samurai and the great military lords who had risen up during the struggles that had destroyed the old families, and raised up new ones.

One of these upstarts was Hōjō Sōun or Ise Naganji, mentioned above, who had originally been a vagrant, then had entered the service of a Daimiō, and finally became an independent general. He conquered two provinces, Izu (1491) and Sagami (1495). His son, Ujitsuna, overthrew the Oyumi Kubō, and extended the conquests made by his father to the provinces of Shimōsa, Kazusa and Awa. His son Ujiyasu overthrew the Koga Kubō and gained the provinces of Musashi, Kōzuke and Shimozuke. And so this Hōjō family which was not related to the well-known Shikken Hōjō family attained supremacy over wide domains in the plain of Kantō.

In the province of Kai, Takeda Shingen distinguished himself by warlike deeds. He conquered the whole of the province of which his father had only possessed small portions, and won for himself also neighbouring districts. In the province of Echigo the warlike Uesugi Kenshin ruled; he pitted himself against Takeda Shingen, and carried on a wearisome war, (1553-1564). They are both famous for the introduction of guns, which had been brought to Japan by Portuguese merchants in 1543. And the Japanese soon left off using bows and arrows, spears and swords.

In the province of Mutsu, Date Masamune, who had formerly been the vassal of a Daimiō, rose to power. He lived in the town of Sendai. He is famous for sending an embassy to Philip III. of Spain, and to Pope Paul V. in 1613.

The Togashi family took the ruling place in the northern provinces. They succumbed, however, in the Shin-Shū,[1] a religious war that broke out among the Buddhists.

The families Amako, Ouchi and Mōri ruled in the west. Ouchi Yoshitaka reigned in the capital, Yamaguchi, which at that time also bore the name of Little Kiōtō. There, in 1550, Francesco Xavier founded a Jesuit settlement. Ouchi Yoshitaka himself embraced Christianity, and worked for its dissemination. But his efforts were ended by the hand of a murderer. Mōri Motonari avenged the deed of violence. After the execution of the murderer, he conquered for himself all the possessions of the Ouchi family. Later he put down the Amako family and so became lord of ten provinces.

Chōsokabe Motochika was all powerful in the island of Shikoku, and in that of Kiūshū the families Shimatsu, Otomo, and Riūzōji won supremacy. Otomo and Riūzōji were Christians and sent embassies to Rome and Spain.

[1] Called also Ikkō-Shū.

In the province of Owari the Oda family rose to power, and they were destined to have a distinguished future. As has been said, Oda Nobunaga put an end to the Ashikaga Shōgunate.

Before relating the further changes in the domestic affairs of Japan through the rise of the Oda family, we shall survey the relations of Japan at this time with foreign lands.

CHAPTER XII

RELATIONS WITH FOREIGN LANDS

THE Mongolian dynasty, the victorious advance of which in China has already been mentioned, reigned there for about 100 years. It was then driven out by a Chinese noble family, Shugenshō, and from 1368 was again confined to their native Mongolia. The Shugenshō founded the new dynasty Ming which reigned till 1661, the year of the foundation of present reigning dynasty of China.

Under the leadership of a powerful noble, named Riseikei, a rebellion broke out at that time in Korea against the reigning dynasty Kō-ryu (Kōrai). In 1392, he founded the Chōsen (or Chōsun) dynasty known later as Kan, which reigned there until the annexation of Korea by Japan in 1910.

As we have seen civil wars were then raging in Japan. It was the period when the imperial family was divided into the northern and southern dynasties. The fighting in Japan and the disorders in China and Korea through the change of dynasty, enabled pirates to pursue their activities unpunished in the south-west, and to gain increasing importance.

They built a powerful war fleet and plundered the coasts of China and Korea. The fleet was well organised. It had flag-ships for the commanders, cruisers, light patrol boats and heavy battleships. It was strengthened by a number of Chinese pirates. They had a harbour for men of war in the island of Kiūsiū; the Japanese "inland sea" served as their headquarters. The governments of China and Korea were powerless against the pirates. Suddenly they appeared and plundered the coasts and the territory situated near the sea, and by the time an army of the government appeared, they had got off with rich booty. The Chinese and Koreans called the dreaded ships butterflies, on account of the long narrow fluttering flags with which they were decorated. They were completely masters of the coasts of China and Korea for more than 200 years, and their power only became weakened in the reign of the Emperor of China, Seisō (1522-1566).

The first Shōgun of the Ashikaga family who was a very zealous Buddhist built a ship in order, for the good of Buddhism, to enter into regular communication with China, and to bring over thence Buddhist books, statues of Buddha and church vessels.

His successors, as we have seen, cultivated relations with China for financial reasons. The 3rd Shōgun, Yoshimitsu, signed himself in letters as the faithful vassal of the Emperor of China, so as to save himself by his help from financial straits.

When the power of the Ashikaga family waned, the Ouchi family which ruled in the town of Yamaguchi (in the province of Suō), continued commercial relations with China and became thereby very wealthy.

It was now that the Portugese and Spaniards who were then masters of the sea and at the zenith of their power, first came to Japan. In 1543 Portugese merchants landed on the island of Tanegashina, and were received in friendly fashion by the Daimiō. They rewarded his hospitality with a gun, which was copied two years afterwards by a Japanese smith, and then brought into general use in the land under the name Tanegashina. Six years later, Francesco Xavier the Spanish Jesuit, landed at Kagoshima in the province of Satsuma. He spread the knowledge of Christianity, and gained many converts; from Kagoshima he went to the island of Hirato, thence to the town of Hakata in the province of Chikuzen, and from there took his way to the town of Yamaguchi in the province of Suō. Everywhere he preached Christianity, and soon there were several Christian churches. He sought the capital, Kiōto, with the intention of converting the Emperor and the Shōgun to his faith. But in consequence of the prevailing disorder and fighting, he met with no success. The spread of Christianity was chiefly in the south-west of Japan. The importance of Portugese and Spanish influence in Japan at that time is shown by the fact that until the present day numerous Portugese and Spanish words have been retained in the Japanese language, e.g. saraca (a towel), savon (soap), capa (macintosh cloak), carta (cards), copo (glass), confetos (a cake), canequim (a towel), etc.

FRANCESCO XAVIER
FOUNDER OF THE JESUIT SETTLEMENT IN JAPAN

PART IV

THE ODA AND TOYOTOMI FAMILIES [1573-1598]

CHAPTER XIII

ODA NOBUNAGA

WE have already stated that after the fall of the Ashikaga family there was no Shōgunate for thirty years. During that time a concentrated and active central government was lacking. The man who then occupied the most powerful position was Oda Nobunaga, who had destroyed the Ashikaga-Shōgunate. He was once more to unite nearly the whole Empire under his rule without attaining the office of a Shōgun.

The Oda family was descended from the Taira. Originally they had been vassals of the Kanriō family, Shiba. Oda Nobuhide, Nobunaga's father, freed his family from that dependent position, and conquered a portion of the province of Owari. It should be noted that he maintained friendly relations with the imperial family. He placed money at the Emperor's disposal, and partly repaired the imperial palace. He was succeeded by his son, Oda Nobunaga, a man of great talents and high ambition. His first military feat was the overthrow of the Daimiō, Imagawa Yoshimoto, who had already conquered three provinces, and was now attempting to destroy the Oda family. After the battle at Okehazama[1] Nobunaga had him beheaded. The victory founded his fame throughout the empire. He then allied himself with Tokugawa Ieyasu who had acquired great power in the east. After the defeat of the Saitō family, he erected a strong fortress in the province of Mino and henceforth resided there.

Some time before, Ogimachi-Tennō had secretly asked him to restore the authority of the imperial throne. Ashikaga Yoshiaki, brother of the Shōgun who had shortly before been murdered through the Matsunaga family, also requested him to take vengeance on the murderers and to appoint him Shōgun. In order to have a free hand for this undertaking, Nobunaga made peace with Takeda Shingen, the most powerful man in the east, and in 1568 marched south to the capital, Kiōto. Soon after his arrival, he overthrew the Matsunaga and Miyoshi families and made Ashikaga Yoshiaki Shōgun. Then he had the imperial palace repaired and instituted a fixed annual income for the Emperor; he also reestablished the court ceremonials which in consequence of the Emperor's poverty had been in abeyance.

Later he was victorious over the Asai and Asakura families at the Anegawa.[2] He burnt the temple of Enriakuji which gave shelter to an army of priests, and thus put an end to the arrogance of the power-

---

[1] Hazama=narrow valley.
[2] Kawa or Gawa=river.

ODA-NOBUNAGA AND HIS SON NOBUTADA

ful Buddhist priests who for five hundred years had recognised no authority over them, and had continually pillaged the land. In order to diminish the secular power of the Buddhist priests, he supported Christianity to which he was himself soon converted.

Ashikaga Yoshiaki whom he had appointed Shōgun was jealous of the growing fame of Nobunaga and thought how he might overthrow him. But Oda Nobunaga got wind of his plans, and sent him into exile, and thus ended the Shōgunate of the Ashikaga family (1573).

A few years later, in 1576, Nobunaga built a strong fortress, seven stories high, called Tenshu, in the province of Omi, on the Biwako.[1] Others soon imitated him, and before long all the greater Daimiōs possessed similar fortresses.

But Nobunaga had not yet attained his goal: the conquest of the whole empire. The Mōri family which had acquired great power in the south-west and owned there 10 provinces especially offered resistance. Nobunaga believed he could reduce them to obedience, and sent his general Toyotomi Hideyoshi against them with a large army, while he himself marched to the east in order to overcome the Takeda family. Hideyoshi was not equal to his task. He tried in vain to take the fortress Takamatsu. He asked Nobunaga for auxiliaries. Nobunaga had been successful, and having destroyed the Takeda, determined to go himself to Toyotomi's assistance

[1] Ko=lake.

with his whole army. On the way to the seat of war, he spent the night in the temple of Honnōji in the capital, Kiōto; he was there attacked by one of his officers, Akechi Mitsuhide. He had been ordered to convey troops to Toyotomi, and thought it was an opportunity to avenge an insult once received by him from Nobunaga. Deprived of all hope of rescue, Nobunaga set fire to the temple, and then killed himself, and his eldest son followed his example. Thus perished this brave and wise man, at the age of 48, when he was just on the point of uniting the whole Empire under his rule (1582).

His death was lamented by his people, but the Buddhist priests rejoiced and declared that his tragic end was Buddha's punishment for his desertion of the ancient faith.

But what Oda Nobunaga had accomplished was not wholly in vain. What he had begun was carried on by his chief officer, Toyotomi Hideyoshi, who was now the most powerful man in the Empire.

TOYOTOMI HIDEYOSHI

CHAPTER XIV

THE CONQUEST AND UNION OF THE WHOLE EMPIRE BY TOYOTOMI-HIDEYOSHI

LIKE so many great men of that time Toyotomi-Hideyoshi[1] was of lowly birth. His father had been a poor peasant. When a boy of fifteen he had volunteered for the service of Oda Nobunaga who, with his keen insight into character, soon recognised his talents and made him a soldier and gradually advanced him to the post of chief officer.

Hideyoshi received the news of his master's death when he lay before Takamatsu, the fortress of the Mōri family. He did not divulge the news, and concluded a favourable peace with the Mōri family. Then he went against Nobunaga's murderer and defeated him at the battle of Yamazaki.[2] Nobunaga's family lived in the castle of Atsuchi, and after the victory negociations took place there between him, the family and the chief vassals, concerning the succession. He effected that the right of primo-

---

[1] His original name was Hiyoshimaru. He received the family name Toyotomi later from the Emperor.

[2] Yama = mountain.

geniture which was firmly rooted in Japan should be adhered to, and that Nobunaga's year old grandson, son of the eldest son who had died with him, should be named successor ; the grown up sons of Nobunaga were passed over. Hideyoshi himself undertook the guardianship of the young heir during his minority.

His powerful position evoked fear and envy, and rebellions soon broke out.

The two most powerful vassals of the Oda family, Shibata Katsuie and Takigawa Katsumasu, first allied themselves against him, and they were joined by Nobunaga's third son. Hideyoshi defeated Shibata Katsuie in the battle of Shizugadake[1] (1583), and pursued him to his castle where he killed himself. Nobunaga's son also killed himself after the battle. Takigawa Katsumasu later surrendered.

Next year, Nabunaga's second son rebelled against Hideyoshi. He was supported in this rising by Tokugawa Ieyasu who with Oda was the most powerful Daimiō. The two armies pitched their camps near Komakiyama.[2] They lay opposite each other for six months without hazarding a decisive battle. There were merely small skirmishes in which Ieyasu had the upper hand. Each of the two generals, Hideyoshi and Tokugawa Ieyasu fully recognised the ability and strength of the other. They became more and more convinced that a decisive battle between them would ruin them both,

---

[1] Dake = mountain.
[2] Yama = mountain.

while allied, they might gain the whole Empire. So a truce was made which soon developed into a friendly alliance, and Hideyoshi adopted Ieyasu's eldest son. Ieyasu subordinated himself to Hideyoshi who treated him always as if he had full equal rights. Each supported the other in all enterprises.

Hideyoshi defeated one after the other, Chōsokabe Motochika, lord of the island of Shikoku, Sassa Narimasa, a Daimiō in the north of the empire and Shimatsu Yoshihisa, a Daimiō of the island of Kiūsiū. Finally he destroyed Odawara, the stronghold of the Hōjō family where they had dwelt for about a hundred years, utterly defeated the family, and took from them the eight provinces of the plain of Kantō that had submitted to them. Thus he ruled the whole of the Japanese Empire (1590).

Hideyoshi had already built himself a splendid palace in the capital. He now had strong fortresses erected at the port of Osaka, and at Fushimi near Kiōtō. The Emperor, who joyfully welcomed the union of the Empire, loaded him with honours and visited him in his palace. Hideyoshi became Kambaku, an office formerly held by the Fujiwara, and Dajōdaijin (first chancellor). He could not attain the ardently desired office of Shōgun, because he was not of noble birth. But that did not injure his powerful position which he tried to strengthen by a new organisation of government. He appointed 5 Bugiō who were responsible to him alone, and the old imperial ministers were as unimportant as ever. He had the whole country surveyed, and instituted new taxes. For the first time after more than 600 years gold and silver coins were minted. Under Hideyoshi's strong hand, order prevailed in the land which had been in a state of anarchy for more than a century.

CHAPTER XV

TOYOTOMI-HIDEYOSHI'S FOREIGN ENTERPRISES

WHEN Hideyoshi found himself the undisputed ruler of the whole Japanese Empire, he made plans for the conquest of neighbouring lands. The desire for conquest and bold enterprises corresponded to the desire for fame and adventure that prevailed at the time. And memories of the pirates' bold deeds whose power had died out, and intercourse with Europeans encouraged men to look beyond their fatherland.

Embassies were sent to Formosa, the Philippines and India to persuade those countries to recognise Japan's supremacy, and everything was prepared for a campaign against China with a view to the conquest of that land. Hideyoshi invited the king of Korea to join him with his army and to act as his guide. The king preferred the supremacy of China, and refused the invitation. Therefore the conquest of Korea became the first objective.

In order to be able to devote himself solely to that enterprise, Hideyoshi transferred the government of Japan to Hidetsugu's nephew whom he had adopted, and made him Kambaku. He himself abdicated, and thenceforth bore the title of Taigō, conferred on a Kambaku who had abdicated.

A large army was assembled in the neighbourhood of the port of Nagoya in the province of Hizen on the island of Kiūsiū. The land troops and the garisson of the fleet comprised together 160,000 men. They went over to Korea from Nagoya. Hideyoshi remained behind with the reserve.

Ukida Hideie was in command of the whole army, Konishi Yoshinaga and Katō Kiyomasa commanded the invading army. The troops under them fought the hostile forces "as easily as bamboos are split," and 20 days after their landing, they marched in triumph into the capital, Seoul. The King of Korea fled to the northwest, to the Chinese frontier, and asked help of the Emperor of China. Konishi pursued him and took the old capital, Phyöng-yang. Katō pursued the two royal princes who had fled to the north-east frontier, and took them both prisoners at Ham-gyung.

The Emperor of China sent a large army under Soshōkun to the king's assistance. But it, too, was speedily conquered by Konishi, and only a few stragglers returned to their native land. A second Chinese army under the command of Yi-yu-Song (Rijioshō) fought at first with real success, and even won a victory over Konishi. But when it attempted to regain the capital, Seoul, the Japanese general Kobayakawa Takakage utterly routed it at Hekiteikan.

After this victory of the Japanese, the Chinese ambassador Shinikei entered into negotiations with Konishi, and he and the Korean ambassador went to

FOREIGN ENTERPRISES

Hideyoshi's court where they agreed to the following preliminary treaty: Japan was to receive half of Korea; a Japanese prince was to marry a Chinese princess, and henceforth there was to be friendly alliance between China and Japan. The two Korean princes were to be set at liberty. But the Chinese envoy did not communicate the articles of the treaty to his Emperor, who after a while sent an embassy to Hideyoshi to make him King of Japan under Chinese supremacy. When the envoy told his message to Hideyoshi, he was exceedingly angry, and prepared a new army to fight against Korea and China.

It landed in Korea in 1596. The campaign led to the famous battles on the mountain of Ulsan, and the brilliant victory of the Japanese at Shi-sen. Katō Kiyomasa, the Japanese general, was besieged by a Chinese army on the mountain of Ulsan. The Japanese suffered terribly from cold and hunger, but notwithstanding they were the victors in the end. The Japanese fleet, too, defeated the Koreans. Unfortunately in 1598 Hideyoshi died. The Japanese army returned home, and these battles which had exacted the greatest sacrifices in life and property during six years, were absolutely unproductive for Japan.

CHAPTER XVI

THE DECISIVE BATTLE BETWEEN THE TOYOTOMI AND TOKUGAWA FAMILIES. VICTORY OF THE TOKUGAWA FAMILY.

THE death of Hideyoshi was naturally of great importance for the relations between the Toyotomi and the Tokugawa families. The good understanding that had existed between them during these last years came to an end.

The Tokugawa family was descended from Minamoto; for many generations they had lived in the province of Mikawa where they had been helpful to the Imagawa family. When the Imagawa were overthrown by Oda Nobunaga, Tokugawa Ieyasu made his family independent, and allied himself with Oda Nobunaga who soon placed great trust in him. At Nobunaga's death Ieyasu already owned 5 provinces. We have seen how war broke out between him and Hideyoshi and how he made peace with him on account of his power and wisdom. When by the overthrow of the Hōjō family, Hideyoshi gained 8 provinces in the plain of Kantō, he presented those to him in place of his former possessions. Tokugawa

VICTORY OF THE TOKUGAWA FAMILY 141

Ieyasu resided at Edo, now Tōkiō. The fame of his virtues increased from day to day.

Shortly before Hideyoshi's death one of the 5 treasurers named Maeda Toshiie was appointed guardian of his son who was a minor. But he only held the post for a short time. After his death Tokugawa Ieyasu was the real head of the government.

Vassals of the Toyotomi family like Ishida Mitsunari and others, were jealous of the growing power of the Tokugawa, and feared that they would once again outshine them and the Toyotomi family. They secretly collected together those minded like themselves and hatched a conspiracy. In 1600 Uesugi Kagekatsu, one of the leaders of the conspiracy, struck the first blow in his native place—Aizu—where he had assembled an army. Tokugawa left one of his officers at Kiōto with a garrison, and proceeded himself with his sons and a large army against the rebels. But on the way he received the news that the vassals of the Toyotomi family had risen in his rear at Osaka, and that the general, Ishida Mitsunari, one of their adherents, was on the point of taking Kiōto. He gave the leadership of the campaign against Uesugi Kagekatsu to his son, and with a portion of the troops hastened himself to the capital. Ishida Mitsunari opposed him with the whole of his army in the plain of Sekigahara. The adherents of the Toyotomi family numbered about 130,000 men, and Tokugawa Ieyasu's army 75,000. A battle ensued in which both sides fought with great animosity. The result of the strife was that one of the leaders of the Toyotomi deserted in the midst of the struggle, and delivered the camp that he commanded to Tokugawa Ieyasu, and with all his forces turned against the Toyotomi. The battle ended in the utter rout of the Toyotomi and Ishida Mitsunari. The latter fled but was captured and killed. Uesugi Kagekatsu soon surrendered. The Toyotomi became the vassals of the Tokugawa; only three provinces remained to them. Tokugawa Ieyasu's heart's desire, that his family should again hold the Shōgunate, was fulfilled.

PART V

THE TOKUGAWA SHOGUNATE

TOKUGAWA IEYASU

CHAPTER XVII

ESTABLISHMENT OF THE TOKUGAWA SHOGUNATE

AFTER the defeat of the Toyotomi the Emperor favoured the victorious Tokugawa Ieyasu. He conferred on him several titles of honour, recognised his descent from the Minamoto, and appointed him Shōgun (1603). Ieyasu made Yedo—the present Tōkiō—his capital and began the internal organization of his newly established rule with the enlargement of the city.

His chief exertions were directed to ensure the lasting possession of the Shōgunate to his family. Therefore he very soon abdicated in favour of his son Hidetada, and made him Shōgun (1605).

But he did not feel confident of the lasting supremacy of his family, so long as the Toyotomi were in possession of considerable power, and he sought for an opportunity to accomplish their destruction. Shortly before his death he attained his desire.

In 1614 he began the war on a trivial pretext. Of the faithful adherents who took up arms for the Toyotomi, Ono Harunaga deserves special mention. Ieyasu and his son, the Shōgun, marched with a large army against the fortress of the Toyotomi at Osaka. Many fierce battles were fought round the stronghold which successfully kept off the enemy's attack. Therefore Ieyasu felt compelled to sue for peace, but with no honourable intention. He was only waiting for the summer in order to begin the war afresh. Accompanied by his son, he again marched with a large army to Osaka, and surprised the garrison. A final fierce struggle ended in the taking of the place by storm. Hideyori, Hideyoshi's son and his mother killed themselves. The victors burnt the fortress to the ground. So ended the Toyotomi family. Tokugawa Ieyasu attained his desire.

The supremacy of his family was assured by the destruction of the Toyotomi, and peace was restored to the land which for more than 200 years had been a prey to incessant wars. For the next 200 years the state both at home and abroad was entirely free from strife.

At the end of his life Ieyasu issued a law concerning the knights containing 13 articles which set forth their position and their duties, and also a decree with 17 articles dealing with court life, and regulating with great detail the court ceremonials, the education and life of the princes, and the duties of the officials of the court.[1]

---

[1] The so-called 100 laws of Ieyasu do not emanate from him. They were the work of Yoshemune, the 8th Shōgun, who in order to lend them a higher authority declared that they had already been written down by Ieyasu, but that he had not proclaimed them.

FORTRESS IN NAGOGA (TOKUGAWA PERIOD)

THE TOKUGAWA SHOGUNATE

The internal organization of the Tokugawa Shōgunate was not finished by Ieyasu. It was only actually settled under Iemitsu, the 3rd Shōgun.

It was essentially more complicated than that of the former Shōgunates. At the head of the whole administration stood the Tairō, the Grand Treasurer, the highest official under the Shōgun. Below him came the board of the 5 Rōchū, the treasurers. They controlled the imperial court officials and Daimiō. Below the Board of the Rōchū was the Board of the Wakadoshiyori[1] the lesser treasurers, comprising from 3 to 5 persons. They had control over the knights. The three departments held regular meetings together under the presidency of the Tairō. Under them again were the three Bugiō in whose hands were the administration of finance, the municipal government of Yedo, and the control of the Buddhist and Shinto temples. The three highest departments of the Kiōto-Shoshidai and the rest of the Bugiō came below them again. They were: the Machi Bugiō of Kiōto (imperial capital), of Osaka (an important port, and formerly the residence of the Toyotomi family), and of Sumpu (residence of the first Shōgun who had abdicated) and the Bugiō of Nagasaki and Sakai (chief towns for foreign trade), of Yamada (town of the celebrated temple of Amaterasu-Omikami), of Nara (formerly the imperial capital), of Nikkō (where the 3rd Shōgun built a temple to Ieyasu in which he enj oye divine honours) etc.

---

[1] Waka=young, Toshiyori or Doshiyori=Rōchū.

Ieyasu reformed the feudal system in a wise and thorough fashion.

The existing Daimiōs, over 260 in number, were divided into three classes. The first formed the Shimpan: they were feudal princes who were related to the Shōgun. The second class formed the Fudai, feudal princes who held their lands as fiefs from the Shōgun. The third class was the Tozama, feudal princes who were brought into subjection by the Shōgunate.

The last class were in the majority. In order to protect himself for ever from their rebellions, Ieyasu settled the Shimpan in the most important districts, e.g. his sons received extensive territories in the provinces adjacent to the two capitals. He always placed the Fudai near the Toyama so that they might act as a guard to the latter, keep them apart, and render rebellion futile. When a noble family became extinct he took possession of their territory as vacant lands.

Later Iemitsu enacted the harsh revolutionary law that the wife and family of every Daimiō must live permanently in the town of Yedo, where they served the Shōgunate as hostages. And each Daimiō had to spend every other year in Yedo with a fixed number of his Samurai. The sojourn there, especially as they had to defray the expenses of their companions was extremely costly for the Daimiō, and led to their impoverishment, a result desired by the Shōgunate in order to preserve peace in the land.

Ieyasu tried to preserve friendly relations with the imperial family. He settled a fixed income on the

Emperor of 10,000 Koku of rice.[1] He and his successors paid him all possible honour, but at the same time took care that he should not acquire any actual power. As has already been said, they appointed a Shoshidai for Kiōto whose duty it was always to watch over the imperial family. The 2nd Shōgun, Hidetada, married his daughter to Gomitsunoo-Tennō. She bore him a daughter who succeeded to the throne as Empress, since Gomitsunoo-Tennō disliked the manner in which the Shōgun oppressed him, and abdicated. The accession of a princess was very rare in Japan. It had not happened for more than 860 years, and now only through the distinguished position of the Tokugawa family which became of still greater importance during the reign of this princess of their blood.

---

[1] About 44 gallons.

CHAPTER XVIII

BUSHIDO

THE establishment of the Tokugawa Shōgunate marks the zenith of the feudal age. We have to survey a period the history of which is almost only the history of the Buke class, of the great military families of the Daimiō and their vassals, the Samurai. The supremacy of that class is most clearly seen in the political organization now introduced by the Tokugawa and which procured a long period of peace, and in the laws which they decreed and administered.

In name the Emperor and the Kuge, the nobility who were his inferiors, still continued to hold a lofty and divine position. But in reality they had no influence in political affairs, were of no importance at all, and spent their lives in strict seclusion.

The people at this time occupied a very subordinate position. All the land, and all the towns belonged to the Shōgun and the Daimiōs. The peasants had to rent the land from them and to pay heavy tribute out of their produce. The inhabitants of the towns, the artisans and merchants, held a still lower place. Neither the peasants nor the townsfolk were

IMPERIAL OFFICIAL (KUGE)
IN COURT DRESS

bondsmen or serfs, but they had very few privileges and very little liberty.

This is the age of the Buke.

In the course of the last centuries so fertile in great struggles and heroic deeds of chivalry, the ruling class of knights was distinguished by its own special code of morals and practical outlook on life, and had evolved a system of ethics of its own known by the term "Bushidō."[1]

Bushidō demanded sincerity and truthfulness from the Samurai. Treacherous actions and crooked ways, lies and duplicity were reckoned a great disgrace. The word of a Samurai was so highly esteemed, that a written promise was held to be unworthy of him.

The Bushi was trained from earliest youth to be courageous, and to endure pain, privation and hardship. The nurse related to the child the great deeds of his ancestors. At night the youth had to visit gloomy spots, places of execution, churchyards, etc., in order to prove his fearlessness. In times of peace, tournaments and jousts in which he could demonstrate his courage formed the chief employment of a Bushi. To yield his life on the field of battle was regarded as supreme happiness and honour.

The knight was not allowed to betray in his face joy, sorrow, or any kind of emotion. It was considered to be incompatible with the absolute self-control that was required of him. To shed tears was reckoned a

---

[1] i.e. way of the Bushi, the knights. Cf. Professor Nitobe's admirable book "Bushido, the soul of Japan," Tokio, 1905.

disgrace. He might not also give expression to his feelings in words, a relief permitted only to poets. The Bushi must not embrace his son in the presence of others, nor kiss his wife. The self-control of the knight is best illustrated by the curious method of suicide among the Japanese.

The suicide of a knight—Harakiri, also called Seppuku and Kappuku—consisted in ripping up the stomach. To kill himself in any other way was disgraceful and unworthy of a knight. A man could only honourably put an end to his life in this painful manner. A knight could even redeem his tarnished honour by Harakiri.

The knight showed absolute equanimity when inflicting on himself this terrible kind of self-murder. As witnessed by European eyes, he grasped his dagger with his left hand without the slightest sign of excitement, drove it in below the navel, on the left side, without changing a muscle of his face, drew it along to the right side, turned it in the wound and made a cut upwards. During the time of the Tokugawas, Harakiri was also used as a punishment. It was considered a great favour if anyone, instead of being executed, was condemned to so honourable a death. Harakiri was a solemn, ceremonial act, executed in the presence of witnesses.

But the knight did not only practice these severe virtues, Bushidō taught him to develop the softer stirrings of his heart.

To love and honour his parents was one of the highest duties of the knight. The Bushi must

SAMURAI AND HIS SERVANT
THE STIRRUP CUP

always be just and fight for the cause of justice. The greatest bravery counted as nothing if the cause was a bad one. The Bushi must have compassion on the weak, the oppressed, and the conquered; it was considered a great disgrace for a warrior to enter into an unequal contest with a younger or weaker adversary and overthrow him.

Above all the knight must be distinguished from an ordinary man by his politeness and refined conduct. He was bound by strict social rules in his intercourse with his fellows which assured the outward expression of sympathetic consideration for the feelings of others. Later, politeness and courtesy came to be regarded by foreigners as a typical Japanese trait. A refined and thorough system of etiquette was practised in knightly circles. The greatest care was taken to learn and to teach how to bow, to walk and sit. Behaviour at meals was a science; tea-drinking was a real ceremonial. The essential quality of the etiquette is expressed in the following sentences by one of its leading spirits: This is the aim of all etiquette: you must learn to demean yourself in such a way that the roughest rascal would not dare to attack your person even if you sit still."

The highest duty of the Samurai was loyalty to his master. He must be ready to give his life for him at any moment. He must even sacrifice the lives of his children for his master's sake.

But it is not to be thought that the relation of the Samurai to the Daimiō was that of a slave to a tyrant. The master was under equal obligation to keep faith with his Samurai, and to care for him as for himself. He was in the position of a father of a family. The obedience of the Samurai was voluntary, not compulsory. It was an unknightly act for a Samurai to execute any order of his lord that did not correspond with his conviction. In such cases he had to warn his master, and try to persuade him. To act against his conscience was not in accordance with the teaching of Bushidō. If the loyalty of a Samurai to his master conflicted with his conscience, his only resource was to commit suicide.

The consciousness of the personal dignity and worth of the Samurai rested on all these virtues, on them rested his honour. Honour was the most valuable possession of the Samurai, and he would joyfully give his life for it. If he injured his honour, he forfeited his existence as a Bushi. Harakiri offered the only means of retrieving his honour.

Apart from Harakiri, the code of honour of the Japanese knight differs most from that of European chivalry in regard to the position of women.

Women held a lower position in Japanese than in European chivalry. While to defend the honour of a woman, to reverence her womanly virtues, and to cultivate purely feminine qualities in her were essential elements in European chivalry, in Japan the woman was trained in warlike courage. She, too, had to learn to control her feelings, to harden her nerves, and to use arms. She learned to swing the Naginata, the long-handled sword, and from early youth was always armed with a dagger (Kai-ken). It was

SAMURAI IN CEREMONIAL DRESS

KNIGHTS EXERCISING

Face p. 155]

considered that this warlike education better enabled a woman to bring up her children to be brave.

This system of ethics soon spread beyond the class of the Buke, and penetrated through the whole nation. Bushidō was the code of honour for all educated Japanese.

The spirit of chivalry and the general culture of the feudal period were of great importance for the future of the Japanese people. It is chiefly due to them that the Japanese were able, later, so quickly to take a place on a level with the rest of the civilized world.

CHAPTER XIX

RELATIONS WITH FOREIGN COUNTRIES

WHEN Tokugawa Ieyasu had firmly established his supremacy over the whole Japanese empire, he did not, like Toyotomi Hideyoshi, think of foreign conquest; he confined himself to depriving the king of Riūkiū of the supremacy he exercised over several small islands in the south of Japan. Otherwise he took care to live in peace with his neighbours, and to encourage commercial relations with them. He brought about a peace between the Daimiō of the island of Tsushima situated near Korea, and Korea, and restored trade with that country. The relations of the two governments were friendly. When a new Shōgun succeeded, the king of Korea sent an embassy to Yedo to offer his congratulations. Ieyasu also sought to set up friendly relations with the Chinese government, but it did not make a ready response, yet all the same, active commercial intercourse arose between Chinese and Japanese merchants.

At this time, too, the Dutch and English first came into contact with Japan; Portuguese and Spaniards

KOREAN EMBASSY

were the only Europeans who had before visited Japan. In 1600 a Dutch ship was driven by contrary winds to Japan. Among others on board were the Dutchman Jan Josten and the Englishman William Adams. Ieyasu gave them a kind reception in Yedo, asked for information about Europe, and kept them at court as advisers. The name of a street in Tōkiō keeps alive their memory to this day. In 1609 a Dutch embassy arrived and with the Shōgun effected the establishment in the name of the Dutch government of regular trade between the two countries, and received permission to build a factory on the island of Hirato. In 1613 the English came, and they also were allowed to build a factory at Hirato. But they found the Dutch competition too strong for them, and soon withdrew, especially as they had discovered a richer field of action in India.

Under the guidance of William Adams, the Japanese learned to build ships in the European manner, and undertook voyages to foreign lands. There arose regular lines of ships to Amakawa, now Makao in China, to Annan, Java, the Philippines, India, etc. In 1610 Japan sent the first ship to Mexico (Nova Hispania), and it soon became usual for Japanese ships to sail the Pacific Ocean.

Motives of religion also took Japanese ships to Europe at this period. Already in 1582 (the 10th Tenshō year) the Daimiōs of Omura, Arima, and Otomo fitted out a ship which sailed through the Indian Ocean and round the Cape of Good Hope to

Spain where these Japanese Catholics paid a visit to Philip II. From Spain they went to Rome and visited the Pope. It was 8 years before they returned to their homes. In 1613 the Christian Samurai, Hasekura Tsunenaga and 6 companions, was sent by his master, Date Masamune, on a voyage to Europe. Contrary to the earlier embassy he sailed over the Pacific Ocean, visited the Governor of Mexico, and then sailed round South America, and across the Atlantic to Spain and Rome. He returned to Japan in the 7th year.

The merchant service was at this time under the charge and protection of the Shōgunate. Every merchant vessel had to carry a certificate of permission from the Shōgunate. They were called Goshuinsen[1] after the certificate.

The love of adventure of the Japanese knights was stirred by long voyages to distant lands, and there are many stories of heroic deeds performed by Japanese adventurers in foreign countries at this time.

Yamada Nagamasa, a knight of the province of Suruga, went to Siam, where already about 8,000 Japanese merchants were living, entered the service of the king, and became commander-in-chief of the Siamese army. On behalf of his master, he conquered a large part of eastern India for the Siamese kingdom. The king gave him his daughter in marriage, and presented him as a fief with a part

---

[1] Sen = ship, Shuin = red stamp, Go = sign of politeness.

of his kingdom. When the king died, leaving a son who was a minor, Yamada Nagamasa became guardian for his brother-in-law, the young king, and as such ruled over the whole kingdom. But the Siamese hated him because he was a foreigner, and poisoned him.

A Rōnin,[1] Hamada Yahei, went with his brothers, and his son and a few Samurai to Formosa in order to take vengeance on the Dutch governor who had continually attacked and plundered Japanese ships. They disguised themselves as peasants and landed, behaving as if they intended to settle there as colonists. They surprised the governor's palace, took him prisoner, seized the valuable treasures, and returned with them to their native land.

Teiseikō accomplished daring deeds in foreign lands, and was the hero of many adventures; his mother was Japanese, his father Chinese. He went to China when the Manchurians made their momentous attack, and the former Chinese imperial family of Ming was overthrown by the Manchurian dynasty of Tsching which still reigns in China. He put himself at the head of the Chinese party of opposition to the new dynasty, and gathered a large number of Chinese troops round him, and from time to time obtained much success. He brought the whole of the country south of the Yang-tse-Kiang into his power, but finally he was compelled to leave China chiefly because the government of the Shōgunate left him without help. He went to the

---

[1] A Samurai who had lost his master.

island of Formosa, expelled the Dutch and made himself king. After his death, he was succeeded by his son and his grandson, and his family governed the island for more than 30 years. But in 1683 his grandson succumbed to a Chinese attack.

In consequence of the missionary efforts of the Jesuits active relations between Japan and foreign lands did not last long.

CHAPTER XX

SPREAD AND SUPPRESSION OF CHRISTIANITY

THE coming of Francesco Xavier to Japan in 1549 resulted in a continuous activity of the Roman Catholic missionaries. Oda Nobunaga, especially, furthered the spread of Christianity. He built a church at Kiōto which quickly became important and was soon recognized as the principal church of the Japanese Christians. It was called Nan Banji. From that time the new faith spread quickly through the provinces adjacent to the capital. Many of the Daimiōs became Christians, and assumed Christian names. The Dominicans, Augustinians, and Franciscans, following the example set by the Jesuits, founded settlements in different parts of the Empire, and carried on their missionary work with great zeal. According to one account the Christians increased to half a million, according to another, even to a million and a half.

But a thorough set back soon occurred.

The Daimiōs, whom the Jesuits had converted to

[1] Nan=southerly, Ban=barbarians, Ji=church.

their faith, became infected with the spirit of the inquisition and began to persecute those of their vassals who refused to become Christians. And therefore they aroused the hatred of the tolerant Japanese people. It seemed almost certain that the Jesuits had it in mind to bring the Japanese Empire under Spanish rule. In any case they awoke the suspicion of Toyotomi Hideyoshi and particularly of the far-sighted Tokugawa Ieyasu, who forbade the farther spread of Christianity.

But the active commercial relations of Japan with Europe rendered it easy for the Jesuits, in spite of the prohibition, to enter the country disguised as merchants and prosecute their activities. Therefore Hidetata, Ieyasu's successor, decided that all proselytizers should be put to death.

Iemitsu, the 3rd Shōgun, finally forbade all commercial intercourse with foreign lands. Portugese merchants were banished for ever. Only the Dutch who carried on no missionary work and were known to be enemies of the Jesuits, were permitted to continue trading. Great cruelty was practised towards the native Christians. They were crucified, burnt, starved, or executed in other sorts of cruel ways by thousands.

The rebellion of the Christians on the island of Amakusa in 1637 was connected with these measures of the government. Masuda Tokisada whose father had been a deadly foe of the Tokugawa family, was the leader of the rising. Masuda Tokisada shared his father's feelings, and at the

JESUITS IN JAPAN

same time cherished the ambition of making himself an independent prince over a larger part of the Empire. In order to gain the people's support, he, by means of all sorts of cunning devices and miracles which he had learned from the Europeans, gave himself out as God, and was supported by the Christians whom he instigated to rise against the hostile Shōgunate. He soon conquered the whole island of Amakusa, allied himself with the inhabitants of the peninsula of Shimabara, murdered its governor and with 37,000 men occupied the fortress of Hara. The Shōgunate sent an army against him under General Itakura Shigemasa. He was unsuccessful, fell later into disfavour, and sought and found death in battle. His successor, Matsudaira Nobutsuna, subdued the rebellious province. Masuda Tokisada was executed, and a terrible massacre of the Christians took place.

After this war, the government took thorough means to prevent the revival of Christianity in the land. Large rewards were publicly offered everywhere for the denunciation of a Christian. The authorities in town and country were ordered to use all possible means of tracking out Christians. If a Christian was seized, two courses were open to him: to return to Buddhism or to die. To the end of the Tokugawa Shōgunate there was a decree in all districts suspected of Christianity that every new born child must, within a fixed period after his birth, trample upon a crucifix. Intercourse with Europe was strictly forbidden. European books were not allowed to be introduced into the land. All the ports were closed. But Nagasaki remained open to the Dutch.

The government made great sacrifices in order to prevent the Christianizing of the country. They sacrificed in most cruel fashion the lives of many subjects, and renounced the advantages accruing from their flourishing trade with foreign lands. They were not actuated by intolerance or by hatred of the foreigner, but believed that they owed these sacrifices to the interests of the state. And in fact it was a matter of the greatest importance for the political life and the civilization of Japan. How different would have been its future if the Jesuits had won over the whole land to Catholicism, and similarly the Christianizing of Japan would have reacted on European affairs.

CHAPTER XXI

THE REIGNS OF IEYASU'S SUCCESSORS. FLOURISHING STATE OF ART AND LEARNING. BEGINNING OF ECONOMIC PROGRESS

IEYASU'S son and grandson were worthy of their predecessor. They were capable rulers and completed the administrative reforms begun by Ieyasu. The government of the 4th Shōgun was also at first very successful, for he had an excellent treasurer. That he, himself, however, was a weak ruler, became evident after the deaths of his trusty counsellors, Matsudaira Nobutsune and Abe Tadaaki. The 5th Shōgun, Tsunayoshi (1681-1709), brother of the 4th Shōgun, showed little interest in or understanding of the task of administration, but he was distinguished for his learning, and promoted art and science.

Under Ieyasu's rule the teaching of Confucius had undergone a revival. His adviser, Hayashi Dōshun, was a zealous advocate of it. Under Tsunayoshi, the fifth Shōgun, Nobuatsu, Hayashi Dōshun's grandson, was appointed Daigaku-no-kami,[1] with the statement

---

[1] i.e. Director of the University of Yedo which bears the name Daigaku.

that the office should become hereditary in his family. So the Daigaku became the headquarters of Confucianism, and produced many famous men. The Confucians were divided into three different schools, the heads of which were respectively Hayashi Daigaku-no-kami, Nakae Tōju and Itō Jinsai.

Science and literature flourished among the followers of Confucius, and were honoured and promoted under the Tokugawa Shōgunate. Keichū, a Buddhist priest, occupied himself with classical Japanese literature; Kitamura Kigin studied mediæval Japanese writings and the Japanese script, and wrote commentaries on Japanese literary works. These studies were the forerunner of a great revival of the classical literature of Japan which was to take a large part in the intellectual and political reorganization of the Japanese nation.

The feudal prince of Mito, son of Ieyashu's youngest son, wrote his " Dainihonshi," i.e., a history of great Japan; it begins with the time of the first Emperor and goes up to Go-Daigo-Tennō, the 96th Emperor, and explains the Japanese forms of government. The work awoke an historical sense, and is, as we shall see, the origin of the movement for restoring the power of the Emperor.

Chikamatsu Monzaimon was a celebrated dramatist of this time. Among the song writers, Matsuo Bashō was most prominent, and he introduced a new metre of lines of seventeen feet into the literature. During the long period of peace, the artistic and serene temperament of the Japanese came more to the front.

Great care was given to fine clothes, beautiful utensils and valuable jewellery. New kinds of amusement were introduced. The Japanese opera Nō came into being, the Japanese *Cabaret*, Jōruri, and the Japanese theatre, Shibai.

Painting flourished exceedingly. Kanō Tanniū, Tosa Mitsuoki, Iwasa Matabei and Hishikawa Moronobu were among the celebrated painters; the two last founded a new school, the Ukiyoe, who took the proceedings of daily life for the subjects of their work, while formerly only landscapes and portraits had been painted. Ogata Kōrin must also be mentioned, after whom the Kōrin school was named.

Yedo, the capital of the Shōgunate, which was becoming more and more a great city, was the centre of political and intellectual life. The Shōguns made good roads from the town out into the country. The 5th Shōgun established a regular line of ships from Yedo to the provinces of Mutsu and Dewa, and he made numerous canals which intersected the city. He also built an aqueduct which provided the town with water from the river Tamagawa.

The river Yodo that flows into the sea at Osaka, was made navigable far inland.

The peace which the Tokugawa Shōgunate gave Japan resulted in the beginning of general economic progress. The people were able to recover from the great exhaustion consequent on the long wars of the Kamakura and Ashikaga period. Yet the reign of the 5th Shōgun was not suited in many respects to forward the development that was going on. His personal merit lay solely in the realms of science and art. The establishment of new lines of communication under his rule is to be ascribed rather to individual officials of capability than to him. He himself took little interest in the business of government. His extravagant court ruined the finance of the state. His need of money led him to have the coins of the Keichō years melted down, and replaced by a new coinage of less value. The new coins which contained only half the amount of real metal of the former ones, decreased in value, and so large classes of the people were injured. His successors therefore won all the more merit in the Japanese Empire.

TOKUGAWA YOSHIMUNE

CHAPTER XXII

THE MOST FLOURISHING PERIOD OF THE TOKUGAWA SHOGUNATE

THE next Shōgun, Ienobu (1709-1712), nephew of his predecessor, made Arai Hakuseki the celebrated scholar and statesman, his adviser. He retained the office with Ienobu's successor. Arai Hakuseki set himself to remedy the principal evil of the government of the 5th Shōgun: the worthless coinage. He gradually called in all the bad coins and had new ones of full value minted. In order to prevent the country from being too much drained of gold and silver by the Dutch, the importation of European goods was limited. He effected that there should be more outward recognition of the dignity of the Shōgunate: that is to say the custom of stating at the ceremony on the reception of the royal ambassador from Korea, that his master held a higher rank than the Shōgun, fell into abeyance. Also by his advice the custom introduced by Ieyasu that only the successor to the throne and the three Miya, the three branch lines of the Imperial house, should found families, and all the rest of the princes and princesses should spend their days in Buddhist monasteries, was abandoned. So Prince Naohitō, son of Higashiyama-Tennō (1686-1709), founded a family of his own, the Kanin-no-miya,[1] from which the present Emperor of Japan is descended.

Ietsugu (1713-1716), the 7th Shōgun, died without issue. The 8th Shōgun was Yoshimune (1716-1745), great-grandson of Ieyasu and son of the Daimiō of Kii. He had a quiet and prosperous reign, preferred a simple court life, and encouraged economy throughout the Empire. He especially sought to check the extravagant life of the Samurai, and to lead their thoughts again to military exercises.

He was zealous to increase the production of the soil. Oranges were cultivated in the province of Kii at this time, tobacco in the provinces of Satsuma and Hidachi, and salt was gathered on the banks of the inland sea; the cultivation of the vine made great advancement in the province of Kai. Yoshimune also planted a kind of potato in the plain of Kantō, and the sugar-cane on the island of Shikoku. He encouraged textile industries, and founded botanical gardens and a sanatorium at Yedo.

He understood men, and recognised talent in his officials. He raised Ooka Todasuke from a subordinate post to be mayor of Yedo (Edo-machi-bugiō) and finally made him a Daimiō. With his help he carried out important reforms in the administration of justice; the so-called 100 articles of Ieyasu are the result of his energy.

[1] Miya = imperial family.

Yoshimune was himself a good scholar; he was a student of astronomy and invented astronomical instruments. He invited Muro Kiūsō, a distinguished student of Chinese literature to his court, and commissioned him to write ethical books for the people. He also sought the society of Ogiū Sorai who was celebrated for his knowledge of Chinese literature. It was at this time of the encouragement of learning that the revival of the classical literature of Japan began with Kada Azumamaro, of which we shall treat later in greater detail. Yoshimune even turned his attention to European culture. He allowed one of his officials at Nagasaki to learn Dutch, and removed the prohibition on the importation of European books. From that time Dutch began to be more and more studied, and thus the influence of European learning began to penetrate gradually into Japan, especially in the departments of medicine and of the arts of war. But Yoshimune feared a closer alliance with Europe, chiefly from conservative leanings, and reverence for the laws of his ancestors. But another cause was fear of a renewal of the missionary activity of the Jesuits and of the conspiracies of Japanese Christians supported by the Catholic powers, and of the Spanish desire for conquest. The Dutch, naturally, did nothing to prevent the exclusion of Europeans, as they greatly desired to keep the Japan trade entirely to themselves.

CHAPTER XXIII

END OF THE GREAT PERIOD OF PROSPERITY OF THE TOKUGAWA SHOGUNATE

The 8th Shōgun, Yoshimune, was succeeded by his son Ieshige (1745-1762). He was sickly and a weak ruler and his reign was marked by many abuses. He was succeeded by his son Ieharu (1762-1786) who left the business of state to his two favourites, the treasurer, Tanuma Okitsugu, and his son Okitomo. Both were avaricious place-hunters who accepted bribes, and farmed the taxes and greatly injured the government and the authority of the Shōgunate. During their reign the land was assailed by dire natural events such as floods, earthquakes, conflagrations and volcanic eruptions. The government took no measures to alleviate the distress, and a universal oppressive famine was the result. Hatred of the two favourites grew more bitter, and at last Okitomo was murdered in the Shōgun's palace, and his father Okitsugu had to abdicate.

Ieharu died without issue in 1786 and was succeeded by Ienari (1786-1838), the grandson of a younger son of Yoshimune.

As Ienari was very young, his relative, Matsudaira Sadanobu, the treasurer, an admirable statesman, governed for him. With his reign Japan entered on a happier period, and as there was then a very clever Emperor, Kōkaku-Tennō (1780-1817), the age is generally spoken of as that of the wise Emperor in the west (Kiōto), and of the clever treasurer in the east (Yedo). Matsudaira Sadanobu carried on the plans and efforts of the 8th Shōgun, Yoshimune. He pursued a policy of economy, and tried particularly to dissuade the Samurai from their extravagant and luxurious way of living, and to induce them to pay their debts. He encouraged science and education, and promoted universities and schools. He kept up good relations with the imperial court, and built a new palace for the Emperor.

He abdicated after 6 years, and Ienari who was now of age, took over the government himself. The Emperor appointed him Dijōdaizin. This was the end of the brilliant period of the Tokugawa Shōgunate.

Famous painters like Maruyama Okio and Katsushika Hokusai flourished at this time. Literature was also of great excellence, especially in the domain of fiction. The people reached a high level of cultivation through a well developed system of elementary schools. That education was soon to prove of great practical importance; the nation was now ripe to take part in the great political questions which were acute at this time.

Ienari abdicated in 1838 after a reign of over 50 years. His descendants were unable to ward off the attacks which had for some time been preparing against the authority of the Shōgunate.

CHAPTER XXIV

THE AWAKENING OF A PUBLIC OPINION. IN-
TELLECTUAL TENDENCIES TOWARDS THE REVIVAL
OF THE IMPERIAL POWER, AND THE OPENING OF
THE COUNTRY TO EUROPEANS

THE revival of learning during the peace that reigned under the Tokugawa Shōgunate, resulted, as we have already indicated, in the renaissance of the old classical literature of Japan. In the time of the 8th Shōgun (1716-1745), Kada Azumamaro awoke interest in the Kojiki, the oldest work of importance, the Homer of the Japanese, in which the divine descent and the first great deeds of the Japanese Emperors were celebrated. His studies were carried on by his pupil, Kamo Mabuchi. But Kamo Mabuchi's pupil, Motoori Norinaga went farther than the others, and his work was the commentary of the Kojiki held now as representative. He there describes the ancient form of government, demonstrates especially how the Japanese imperial family has reigned uninterruptedly from the earliest times, and he awoke the consciousness of the Japanese people to the ancient honour and dignity of the imperial dynasty. He had a distinguished pupil, Hirata Atsutane, who was the reformer of the old ancestor-worship which from

REVIVAL OF THE IMPERIAL POWER 175

this time onward was called Shintoism. These four men were called the four Ushi[1] of Shintoism. Their writings were very widely read, and they found everywhere enthusiastic disciples and pupils.

This activity in matters of historical learning had great practical results. The opinion became general that the Emperor must be restored to his ancient power and position, and that the authority of the Shōgunate which really rested on usurpation, must be destroyed. To advocate this course the historian Rai Sanyō wrote his " Nihongaishi " (Japanese private history).[1] The book deals with feudal history from the Kamakura period to the Tokugawa Shōgunate, and is very hostile to the feudal system. The work was eagerly read and understood. Everyone knew that Rai Sanyō's attacks on the Minamoto and the Taira really pointed at the ruling Tokugawa, and so the discontent with the prevailing régime increased every day.

Two Samurai of low rank, Takeuchi Shikibu and Yamagata Daini, attempted to set on foot a practical reorganization of the present conditions. Under the 9th Shōgun, Takeuchi Shikibu went to Kiōto, and tried to induce the imperial court officials to make use of public opinion and shake off the authority of the Shōgunate. The government at Yedo saw through his plot, and sent him into exile. Under the 10th Shōgun, Yamagata carried on the plan, and the

[1] Great men.
[2] History written by a private individual, in contrast to the official histories.

Shōgun made him pay with his life for his alliance with Takeuchi and others of a similar way of thinking. But even these strong measures could not protect the Shōgunate from the prevailing efforts. Men arose in all parts of the Empire who carried on a violent agitation, and urged the people to rise against the Shōgunate.

Another intellectual tendency was associated with that "public opinion" which was directed against the government of the Shōgunate, and had its part in undermining its authority. It has been told how from 1637 fear of the Jesuits' activity and of the Spaniards' desire of conquest had caused the exclusion of Europeans from Japan. Nagasaki alone had remained open to the Dutch, and the 8th Shōgun had permitted the Japanese to learn the Dutch language, and allowed the introduction of Dutch books. Dutch physicians in Nagasaki taught numbers of Japanese. Those Japanese students soon formed an influential party, which adopted European customs, and were enthusiastic at the idea of introducing an European system of education.

The relations of Japan with Europe soon became a burning question. In 1786 the Russians who had already taken possession of the whole of Siberia came to the north of Japan, to the island of Ezo (Hokkaidō) that belonged to it, and conquered several small islands. The Shōgunate government were again seized with fear of European plans of conquest, and fortified the coast in the neighbourhood of Yedo. They sent several expeditions to gain information about the northern districts and frontiers of the Empire. One of them was led by Mamiya. He discovered incidentally that Saghalien which had hitherto been regarded as a peninsula, was an island, and therefore the straits between Saghalien and the mainland were named the Mamiya Straits. He led his expedition as far as Manchuria, and the information he obtained there is set down in the narration of his travels. At that time, too, Inō-Chūkei made the first map of Japan. The Russians repeated their attacks on the island of Ezo, and the English landed in Kiūsiū, and in 1808 burnt a village near Nagasaki. Such events served to strengthen the Shōgunate in its principle of excluding foreigners, and as a number of European merchants penetrated inland from Nagasaki, in 1825 the order went forth to the Daimiōs to expel all Europeans.

Then the students who had learned Dutch and adopted Dutch civilization, made themselves heard. They declared that in order to defend themselves successfully from European attacks, they must enter into closer relations with Europe. Watanabe Kazan and Takano Chōei wrote several books promulgating that view. The government forbade their publication and imprisoned their authors; Takano Chōei had to kill himself. But their ideas could not be suppressed and spread even in the circles of the Shōgunate itself, for the foreign powers who urged more and more the opening of the country, convinced them of the superiority of their civilization and especially of their arms.

CHAPTER XXV

CONCLUSION OF THE FIRST COMMERCIAL TREATY

THE 11th Shōgun abdicated in 1838, and was succeeded by his son Ieyoshi (1838-1853). In the beginning of his reign the treasurer, Mizuno Tadakuni, attempted to carry out domestic reforms which aimed at strengthening the power of the Shōgunate. But they failed completely, and led to the fall of the minister.

His successor was Abe Masahiro, and on him fell the task of deciding the foreign question. In July 1853 four American ships sailed into the harbour of Uraga in the province of Sagami. Their commander, Admiral Perry, asked the Shōgun in the name of the United States to make a commercial treaty. The Shōgunate was uncertain, and asked to be allowed to consider the matter until the next year. Two months later a Russian ship sailed into the harbour of Nagasaki, and a Russian envoy asked in the name of his government for the conclusion of a commercial treaty. In his uncertainty, the treasurer applied to the imperial court officials and the Daimiōs. The court officials and a large majority of the Daimiōs were unanimous for continuing to exclude foreigners. Public opinion was greatly excited by these negociations. It was clear that a large majority of the people, and especially the imperial party, were against the foreigners. But, notwithstanding, the government did not venture to give the American embassy an absolute refusal. They feared that it might lead to serious quarrels with foreign powers, and even to the conquest of the whole country. In order to find some way out of a difficult position, they decided to open to the Americans the two worst harbours in the country, Shimoda in the province of Izu, and Hakodate in the island of Ezo (or Hokkaidō). A provisional treaty was made with Perry, 31st March, 1854, who had reappeared with a flotilla of seven ships, at Uraga. Treaties soon followed with Russia, England and Holland, and the same ports were opened to those countries.

These measures of the government called forth a storm of indignation from the people, especially from the imperial party who sought to make use of the general dislike of foreigners and the Shōgunate for the attainment of their goal: the restoration of the imperial family to its original position of power. The small party friendly to the Europeans which was utterly opposed to the imperial party possessed too little actual power for the Shōgunate to find their support of real help.

The Shōgun was Iesada, son of the 12th Shōgun who had died in 1853. His aged treasurer, Abe Masahiro, felt no longer able to support the tasks awaiting the government and resigned. His successor was the Daimiō, Hotta Masahiro, who belonged to the European party and was in favour of opening all the trading ports. When in 1856 the United States sent a consul in the person of Harris Kam with the commission to obtain a definitely better treaty of commerce, Hotta Masahiro received him as he wished at Yedo, and introduced him to the Shōgun in person, a proceeding quite at variance with prevailing custom. He, moreover, appointed a commission for the purpose of working out a treaty of commerce, which held its meetings in the Shōgun's palace. In 1858 a treaty was concluded with the United States by the articles of which the best ports were opened to them, and which remained the basis for all commercial treaties with that power until 1904.

The principal articles of the treaty were :—

1. Japan and the United States of America were henceforth to cultivate friendly relations with each other.

3. Besides the ports of Shimoda and Hakodate, the following ports were to be open to the United States: Kanagawa (Yokohama), 4 July, 1859; Nagasaki, 4 July, 1859; Niigata, 1 January, 1860; Hiōgo (Kōbe), 1 January, 1863. Shimoda was closed 6 months after the opening Kanagawa.

4. The Japanese government to levy duties on imports and exports.

THE FIRST COMMERCIAL TREATY

6. The Americans to be under the jurisdiction of their own consular courts, and not under the Japanese courts of law.
7. The Americans to move freely in the neighbourhood of the open ports in a space of about 25 miles.
8. Religious tolerance to be extended to the Americans in the regions open to them.
9. The Japanese government to extradite American criminals.
10. The United States to be willing to sell ships of war, steamers and arms to the Japanese government, and to place at its disposal instructors, officers and artisans.
14. The treaty to be valid from 4 July, 1859.

In order to be legal, the treaty required the signature of the Emperor. But at that time the imperial capital, Kiōto, was the seat of the chief leaders of the imperial party. They zealously worked for the removal of the Shōgunate, and sought to make opposition to the foreigners serve their purpose, while for their part they supported the entire exclusion of foreigners. The Emperor refused his signature, although Hotta Masahiro asked for a personal audience. Therefore Hotta resigned.

His successor, Ii Naosuke, a courageous and talented man, fully shared his predecessor's convictions. In 1858 he finally concluded the treaty of commerce dispensing with the Emperor's signature, and opened the ports agreed upon to the United

States. He soon made similar treaties with Russia, England, Holland, France and Prussia, likewise against the desire of the Emperor.

Therefore he was the best hated man in the Empire. It chanced that the young Shōgun died just then. The Lord High Treasurer summoned the next heir, the 13 year old grandson of the 11th Shōgun, from the province of Kii, and made him Shōgun. This proceeding of Ii was violently attacked by the Daimiōs. It was thought to point to a desire for sole authority, and that for that purpose he had made a Tokugawa, who was a minor, Shōgun. The vassals and friends of the Daimiō of Mito who was a Tokugawa, and whose family had long possessed the hereditary title of Vice-Shōgun, specially agitated against the Lord High Treasurer, and tried to make Tokugawa Yoshinobu, the grown-up son of the Vice-Shōgun, Shōgun. As he belonged to the imperial party, he won strong support. A conspiracy was formed between the imperial court officials, and the Daimiōs who belonged to the imperial party, for the purpose of driving out all foreigners through the Vice-Shōgun. But Ii discovered the plot, took the chief leaders prisoner, and condemned them to incarceration; on some of them the sentence of harakiri was passed. These severe measures only served to increase the hatred borne him. The following year, 1860, he was murdered by Samurai at the Sakurada gate as he was about to enter the Shōgunate palace.

Samurai and Rōnin, hostile to the Shōgunate, also

made numerous attempts against foreigners at this time.

Ii's successor, the treasurer Andō Nobumasa, continued a policy of friendly relations with Europeans. But recognising the weakness of the Shōgunate, he thought of reconciliation with the imperial court. In 1862 he sent an embassy to Europe and America to negociate a delay in the time fixed for the opening of some of the ports. He married the young Shōgun to an imperial princess, and by so doing increased the bitter hatred of his enemies. He was attacked and seriously wounded in the Shōgunate palace.

Thus the imperial party were successful in using the complications that arose out of the foreign policy to bring about the fall of the Shōgunate.

CHAPTER XXVI

FALL OF THE SHOGUNATE. RESTORATION OF THE IMPERIAL POWER

MEANWHILE a large number of Daimiōs and Samurai who were discontented and inclined to the imperial party, had gathered in the imperial capital, Kiōto. They criticised openly and severely the government of the Shōgunate. Foreign policy came in for a large share of blame, and they demanded the overthrow of the Shōgunate, and the restoration of the legitimate imperial government. The imperial court officials naturally sympathized with these views. In 1862 in the name of the Emperor they invited the Shōgun to come to Kiōto, to drive out the foreigners, and to carry out various reforms, especially that of the Shōgunate government. The Emperor ordered the Daimiōs to drive out all foreigners.

Naturally the Shōgun did not obey, but he had no power to prevent the imperial party from proceeding against foreigners. The American and the English embassies at Yedo were burnt down. By order of the Daimiō of Nagato (Chōshū) an American ship was fired at from the Bakan fort, 10th May, 1803, a

French ship, 23rd May, a Dutch one, 26th May, an American, 1st June, and a French, 5th June, when passing through the Bakan straits. His act resulted in the bombardment of the Bakan fort, 5th-8th August, 1863, by a fleet consisting of 9 English, 3 French, 1 American and 4 Dutch men of war. The fort was taken, and the Daimiō was compelled to sue for peace. The confederate powers demanded as indemnity three million pounds sterling from the Shōgunate government. It paid the sum in order to avoid a dangerous war.

The year before, 1862, an Englishman named Richardson was murdered by the retainers of Shimatsu Saburō, brother of the Daimiō of Satsuma, while accompanying him on his return from Yedo, because he had not paid the prince the customary homage. When the English were informed of the murder, they demanded that Shimatsu Saburō should be delivered up to them. As this was refused, their fleet, in July, 1863, bombarded and destroyed Kugoshima, the port of the princedom of Satsuma. Satsuma sued for peace and declared itself willing to pay the heavy sum of £25,000 demanded by the English as compensation. The Shōgunate made its apologies for the occurrence, and paid £100,000 as idemnity.

If then war was avoided by the sensible policy of the Shōgunate, a greater danger was threatened by the ultra-imperial party which ruled the Emperor's court and the imperial capital and surrounding territory. In its blind hatred of the foreigner it would have plunged the country into the greatest perils had not the Shōgunate warned the Emperor of the dangerous doings of those people, and so brought about a change in the imperial policy towards foreigners.

Matsudaira Katamori, prince of Aizu, a relation and adherent of the Shōgun, a man of education and enlightment, and a friend of Europe, went to Kiōto and allied himself with the imperial court. He gained the help of a prince of the imperial family. Through him the Emperor was informed of recent events, and was shown how dangerous it was to continue the policy of hostility to the foreigner, and how much wiser it would be to encourage friendly intercourse which would be advantageous to the well-being of the country. His warning did not fail to have effect. The Emperor recognized that he must change his policy in regard to the foreigner, if he did not wish to bring great disasters on the whole empire. He was ready to take on himself the responsibility and the consequences with regard to the Shōgunate on the one hand, and the ultra-imperial party on the other. In September, 1863, he sent the prince of Nagato, an extremist of the imperial party, into exile. Seven imperial court officials who had supported Nagato, had to flee. The prince of Satsuma supported this important change in the imperial policy, made an alliance with Matsudaira Katamori and entered into friendly relations with various foreigners. The Emperor even determined to make use of the military power of the Shōgunate. He transferred the custody of the imperial capital and of the imperial palace, Matsudaira

Katamori, to his Shōgunate troops and his ally, the prince of Satsuma. In 1865 against the will of the imperial government, he acknowledged the treaty of commerce that had been made by the Shōgunate in 1858 with foreign powers. The imperial court itself entered into friendly relations with individual Europeans. The prince of Satsuma successfully convinced many Daimiōs how unfounded was their dislike of the foreigner. Hatred of the foreigner decreased more and more in the imperial party, especially when the embassy sent to Europe and America in 1862 returned, full of praise of European civilization. It seemed as if the continuance of the Shōgunate's authority was assured, since it had once more gained a remarkable victory in the domain of diplomacy.

But the Daimiō of Nagato was its implacable enemy; he was meditating revenge for his exile that had been effected by Matsudaira Katamori. His vassals undertook in July, 1864, an attack on the imperial capital that was only overcome with difficulty by Matsudaira Katamori and the Daimiō of Satsuma. When in June, 1866, the Shōgunate sent an army against Nagato in order to crush him finally, it was seen how greatly the military power of the Tokugawa was weakened. The troops could do nothing, and had to return without having accomplished their mission, a circumstance that meant injury to the position of the Shōgunate.

The Shōgun died in August, 1866, and the Emperor in December of the same year. The

Shōgun's successor was Tokugawa Yoshinobu, son of the Vice-Shōgun at Mito. The present Emperor Mutsuhito ascended the imperial throne in 1867.

The almost simultaneous deaths of the Emperor and the Shōgun were a cause of weakness in the political situation, and the leaders of the imperial party felt they must use it for the prosecution of their aims.

In 1865 the two most powerful vassals of the Daimiō of Satsuma, the knights Saigō Takamori and Okubo Toshimichi, both holding the views of the imperial party, had entered into a secret alliance with a vassal of the prince of Nagato, the Samurai Kido Takayoshi. They planned that Nagato should again join with Satsuma, and that both together should abolish the Shōgunate, and restore the Emperor to his old power. The 15th Shōgun, Tokugawa Yoshinobu, was as we have seen, a supporter of the Emperor. He now had to deal with foreign affairs, and thought it best in so difficult a situation to avoid civil war, and sympathising with the imperial party would not enter into a struggle on behalf of the Shōgunate with the Emperor. By the advice of the Daimiō of Tosa he delivered a written document to the Emperor, 19th November, 1867, in which he declared that he would place the government of the Shōgunate in the Emperor's hands. The document that forms so important a turning point in the history of Japan runs as follows:

"Since the middle ages the imperial power has been more and more diminished through the Fujiwara family. Later Minamoto Yoritomo assumed the position of a Shōgun, and brought the power of the government into the possession of the Shōgunate. I regret that so many obstacles are in the way of my administration of the office. Foreign affairs play an ever larger part, and intercourse with foreign countries is continually on the increase. The time therefore demands that our country should have one united government. Herewith I give my power back into your majesty's hands. Only when the Emperor shall rule over the whole land, unite all classes under his government and guard our fatherland, can our nation compete with foreign states. I thus fulfil my duty to king and country."

And so after a *fainéant* existence of 683 years, the Emperor again entered on the actual possession of the government.

All honour must be accorded to the policy of the Shōgunate from the time of Perry's appearance when the question of relations with foreign countries entered on a new stage. Its policy was guided solely in the interests of the state. The Shōgunate did not make the treaty of commerce from love of the foreigner but from conviction of the superiority of foreign powers, and of the danger of quarrelling with them. The Shōgunate, from a feeling of responsibility for the fate of the Empire, acted against the will of the people and of the imperial court, and so undermined its own power. From the same point of view of the best interests of the state, the last Shōgun determined to avoid civil war and voluntarily to place his office in the Emperor's hands.

FOURTH PERIOD

MEIJI

CHAPTER I

BEGINNING OF THE MEIJI AGE

AT the time of the last Shōgun's resignation, the new Emperor was only fifteen years old, and his councillors of the imperial party decided all matters of state. Their policy was to secure the supremacy of the imperial party throughout the empire, and to render nugatory any attempt at a future restoration of the Shōgunate. Their first act was to replace the Shōgunate troops to whom the custody of the imperial palace and capital were entrusted by a strong imperial army. For this purpose peace was concluded with the Daimiō of Nagato with whom there had been war in consequence of the change of imperial policy in 1863, and who had a large military force at his disposal. In December, 1867, Matsudaira Katamori was ordered to withdraw with his troops from the imperial palace. Its custody was transferred to the Daimiōs of Satsuma and Tosa and their friends. Terms of peace were offered to the Daimiō of Nagato, and he was asked to come to the capital with troops. The seven imperial court officials who had fled were recalled and reinstated in their offices. The official imperial proclamation relating to the new order of administration was published, 3rd January, 1868. It officially put an end to the former Shōgunate government, and it was solemnly declared that for the future all power was vested in the Emperor. The imperial bureaucracy was newly organized. The Sōsai (president) and under him the Gijō (lesser council) and the Sanyo (greater council) formed the head of the imperial officials. The Sōsai was Prince Arisugawa-no-miya Taruhito, an uncle of the Emperor, the members of the lesser council were princes and Daimiōs belonging to the imperial party, especially those of Satsuma, Tosa, and Nagato, and of the greater council Samurai of the imperial party. None of the former Shōgunate officials received a post. The ex-Shōgun, several of the Tokugawa, and Matsudaira Katamori were entirely passed over when the offices were filled.

Tokugawa Yoshinobu and his adherents naturally felt the ingratitude of such conduct on the part of the imperial government, and were extremely angry. Yoshinobu was then in the Shōgunate palace at Kiōto, and here too had come Matsudaira Katamori after his withdrawal with his troops from the imperial palace. The troops themselves were so deeply stirred at the injustice shown their commander that Yoshinobu feared they might attack the imperial palace and so revenge themselves on the imperial party. In order to prevent bloodshed, notwithstanding that he was himself much offended, he marched with all his troops to Osaka.

THE MEIJI AGE

The imperial party who expected nothing good of Yoshinobu summoned him in the name of the Emperor to return to the capital without his army; he would be received in a friendly way and could lead an honourable life at the imperial court.

Discord prevailed in Yoshinobu's camp. Yoshinobu inclined to the preservation of peace, and was not unwilling to accept the imperial offer. Matsudaira Katamori, on the contrary, urged an attack on the capital, and the destruction of the imperial party at court. In the end Yoshinobu marched to the capital with his whole army.

The princes of Satsuma, Nagato and Tosa waylaid him at Fushimi, where fighting took place, 28th January, 1868, in which the Shōgunate troops were defeated. They were superior in numbers but the situation became daily more unfavourable for Yoshinobu. Prince Ninnaji-no-miya Yoshiaki took over the chief command of the imperial army. For the first time he again bore the insignia of an imperial general: Kinki, the brocade banner, and Settō, the sword of justice. The Shōgunate soldiers became more and more conscious that they were rebels, and the number of those who refused to take up arms against their Emperor continually increased. Yoshinobu marched back to Osaka with his army where he disbanded it, and fled by sea to Yedo.

On February 5th, the imperial government published a proclamation declaring Tokugawa Yoshinobu and all his adherents rebels, and depriving them of all rights and honours. Prince Arisugawa-no-miya Taruhito now became commander-in-chief of the imperial army, and marched with it to the east.

Yoshinobu was tired of the struggle. He repaired to the temple of Kaneiji in order to testify his peaceable and loyal state of mind, and implored Arisugawa to obtain his pardon from the Emperor. The imperial army entered Yedo on April 26th and occupied the Shōgunate palace without striking a blow. Yoshinobu's life was spared, and he was exiled to his native Mito. As his successor in the royal house of Tokugawa, the imperial party appointed the young Tokugawa Iesato.

But the civil war was not at an end. A number of the Shōgun's loyal vassals who called themselves Shōgitai, true union, occupied the park of the temple of Kaneiji at Yedo, and appointed Prince Rinoji-no-miya, a Tokugawa, the former high priest of the temple, their commander-in-chief. A fierce battle was fought in the park, on July 4th, in which the imperial party were victors. The temple with its valuable art treasures was almost entirely destroyed. The Shōgitai fled to the territory of Matsudaira Katamori in the north of the Empire where the struggle was continued. Matsudaira won the adherence of 22 other Daimios of northern Japan, and gave the government a great deal of trouble for more than 6 months.

After defeating the Shōgitai, the imperial army turned its attention to the provinces of Shimōsa and Shimozuke where Otori Keisuke, an adherent of the Shōgunate, was making a stubborn resistance. After several battles, only one of which ended favourably for the Shōgunate cause, Otori fled to the town of Aizu where the prince of that district, Matsudaira Katamori and the Daimiōs allied with him, had collected their very considerable forces.

The town of Aizu is situated on the tableland of Aizu which is surrounded on all sides by high mountains, and difficult of access to an attacking party. The imperial troops marched by two ways to the tableland: one division went through the province of Echigo along the river Aga-no-gawa which rises in the Aizu tableland, and on the banks of which the town of Aizu is situated; the other marched by the hostile fortress, Shirakawa, and took it. In the beginning of October the imperial troops commenced an attack on the town of Aizu. Matsudaira's adherents made a stubborn resistance. The Biakko-Tai, an association of youths from 15 to 17 years old who had joined together for the purpose of defence, deserves special mention. They fought with great courage; 19 of them, when the town perished in flames, ended their lives by Harakiri. A few women, armed with spears, took part in the battle. In the end the imperial army was victorious. Matsudaira, wishing to save the lives of the 3000 besieged, forbade suicide, and surrendered with them to the conquerors who exercised mercy. The Daimiōs, his allies, who were scattered through the land, gradually surrendered.

The war was also carried on at sea. The

Shōgunate had acquired a number of men-of-war built in Holland, 8 of which were in the hands of Enomoto Takeaki, a faithful adherent of the Shōgunate. These ships succumbed to the imperial fleet in the battles at the port Miyako and at the island of Ezo. There the fortress Goriōkaku made a long resistance and only surrendered in July, 1869. That event ended the civil war, and ensured the imperial supremacy throughout the land.

Meanwhile the government had come to a firm decision in regard to the question of foreigners. Now that the whole responsibility of government lay with the imperial party, they considered it incumbent on them to be on friendly terms with foreign powers. Even men like the Prince of Nagato who had a few years ago violently agitated for the exclusion of foreigners, now agreed to the policy of friendly relations with them. It became clear that the hostile position of the imperial party towards foreigners had been essentially due to their opposition to the Shōgunate. The prejudices, too, which had actually prevailed with them, disappeared in closer intercourse with the Europeans who at this time came in large numbers to the country. The imperial court was now not only convinced that the entire opening up of the country was an absolute necessity, and that it would bring misfortune on the whole empire to resist the superior force of foreign nations, but also hoped to derive advantage from the adoption of European forms of civilization.

The Emperor on February 7th, 1868, the first Meiji

year, sent an embassy to the representatives of the foreign powers at Hiōgo (Kōbe) to inform them that the Shōgunate government no longer existed and that the Emperor alone held authority: the imperial government had instituted a special office for foreign affairs and desired henceforth to maintain friendly relations with foreign powers. It did not rely merely on these promises; the government proved by deeds how much it was in earnest. When the Rōnin (errant knights belonging to no lord) or the regular troops made attacks on Europeans, severe measures were taken against the evil-doers, and the government did not hesitate to risk the displeasure of their own vassals. Twenty knights of the Prince of Tosa who had killed a French officer with eleven men were condemned to carry out harakiri in a Buddhist temple at Sakai in the presence of the French ambassador; the last 9 of them, at the request of the ambassador who was unable to endure the terrible spectacle any longer, were let off with banishment.

A few days after the transmission of the imperial declaration to the representatives of the foreign powers at Hiōgo, the Emperor Mutsuhitō solemnly read a proclamation to the highest Kuge and Daimiōs in the temple belonging to the imperial palace at Kiōto, and ratified it with his oath. The proclamation contained the guiding lines of the future imperial policy.

1. Assemblies shall be called into being in which all classes of the people shall be represented. All affairs of state shall be therein discussed and public opinion will thus find expression.

2. In future all distinction between the upper and lower classes of the people shall as far as possible be removed for the purpose of securing the order and peace of the Empire.

3. Every individual, the highest officer of the state as well as the most insignificant man of the people, shall strive to do his work well and not neglect his special calling.

4. Old-fashioned and useless manners and customs shall be banned, and efforts made to guide the people in right directions.

5. Knowledge from all parts of the world shall be made use of for rendering the state strong and secure.

On November 6th, 1868, the Emperor followed the old custom of naming the new era. He called it Meiji, i.e. "brilliant or shining reign." He decided that for the future such a designation should hold good for the whole reign of an Emperor.

At the end of 1868, the official machinery that had been set up on January 3rd was again abolished and its place taken by provisional offices. In July, 1869, an organization of the imperial central government was set up on the model of the administrative reforms of the first Taihō year. A Jingikan and a Dajōkan were again appointed, of which the last comprised the Dajōdajin or Chancellor-in-chief, the Sadaijin or Chancellor of the left and the Udaijin or Chancellor of the right. As we said above, single ministerial departments were under the Dajōkan which

THE MEIJI AGE

resembled the modern European ministries. Corresponding to that model, six ministers were appointed under the Dajōkan : a minister of the imperial family, a minister of finance, a minister of foreign affairs, a war minister (from 1872 minister of war and the marine), a minister of justice, and a minister of home affairs. The Jingikan was abolished and replaced by a minister for religion under the Dajōkan.

These offices were bestowed on the most meritorious knights of the imperial party ; only one of the princes, the prince of Satsuma, received an office, and he was appointed Chancellor of the left.

The Emperor fixed his residence at Yedo, November 26th, 1868, and from that date it bore the name Tōkiō, i.e. the eastern capital.

The Shōgunate was at length at an end and the imperial power restored. But even so, the restoration was only partial. It did not yet possess by a long way such a position as the Taika reforms had given it, or at least attempted to give it. There were still 277 Daimiōs who only acknowledged the imperial supremacy, and possessed all the power and authority that a German confederate prince has to-day, and besides had undiminished rights of maintaining their own Samurai army.

But, through the great enthusiasm for the new imperial government these conditions, also, came to an end. A number of ministers requested the Daimiōs under whom they had hitherto been as Samurai, to give up their independent position as princes, and to place their lands in the Emperor's hands. Among them were the Daimiōs of Nagato, Satsuma, Tosa, and Hizen, and they prepared a document to be signed and presented to the Emperor in which it was stated:—

"Formerly the imperial family alone held the reins of government, and so should they govern in the future. The whole Empire must be governed by our Emperor, since the land belonged to him from the beginning, and all the people are his subjects. Our vassals cannot live a single day without the Emperor. In the middle ages the Kamakura Shōgunate violently bereft the Emperor of his power. The Tokugawa Shōgunate and ourselves did not realise the wrong we were doing. But now we repent, and are prepared to give our lands back to the Emperor. Only if our Empire is united under one ruler will it be able to compete with the European states." Gradually the signatories to this document were able to persuade many other Daimiōs to give up their independence and their lands.

The imperial decree that put an end to the feudal system followed on June 17th, 1869. The decree abolished the princely power of the Daimiōs; all lands became the property of the Emperor, and all the Japanese, his subjects. The independent powers which the feudal system had created came to an end, and one central power governed the whole Empire and all its inhabitants. The decision meant an absolute change in the political, social, economic, and intellectual life of the nation, the importance of which was incomparably greater than the speedy introduction of the technical achievements of European nations, a striking circumstance that chiefly attracts attention, but it was really a result of the sweeping political reforms. The former feudal subjection was replaced by civil liberty, intellectual enlightenment, and a wholly new economic life. The complete destruction of the petrified political forms of the old feudal system was an essential factor in the adoption in its widest extent of European civilization.

But the ethical advantages of feudal times were not destroyed by the abolition of the political forms of the feudal system. Bushidō still continued to exist; the chivalrous ideas, especially the lofty sense of honour of the Japanese acquaintance with which we have made in feudal times, played an essential part in the wonderful success of the Japanese nation in its thorough and speedy adoption of the advantages of European civilization. The sense of honour that made the nation unable to endure being looked down on, was calculated in a high degree to determine the Japanese eagerly to adopt the new methods. But it was not only by its moral qualities that the Japanese nation so quickly won the esteem of Europe: even more important was the fact that it was sufficiently educated both intellectually and aesthetically to appreciate the superiority of European civilization. We have pointed out the great epochs of the intellectual and artistic activity of the Japanese nation, and have mentioned great scholars and artists who before the closer ties with Europe did distinguished work. There were a large number of institutions for higher education; there were elementary schools in all the larger communities. The difficult art of writing was practised by the greater part of the people. That Japan did not earlier enter into relations with Europe had its cause in its historical development, in its domestic politics. An absolute change in those politics was required, and the decree of June 17, 1869, brought it into being.

With the revolution that removed all the Daimiōs and Samurai from their former position was bound up the question of what was to be done with them in the future. The decree of June 17, 1869, appointed the Daimiōs as prefects and territorial governors over the lands they had formerly possessed. Compensation in money was given to the Samurai. But in 1871 the imperial government dismissed all the Daimiōs from their offices, and compensated them with money paid in government bonds. The amount differed in accordance with the importance of each prince. The whole sum paid in compensation to the Samurai and Daimiōs was about £17,390,000. The government in addition undertook to pay all the princes' debts, a sum of not less than £1,743,229.

Their titles were fixed on this occasion. All the Daimiōs and former imperial court officials received the appellation of Kazoku, i.e. Flower or noble families. They resided almost without exception at Tōkiō. The families fell into five classes according to their former importance: 1. Kō = prince, 2. Kō (written in Japanese differently from the first Kō) = marquis, 3. Haku = Earl, 4. Shi = viscount, 5. Dan = Baron. There

THE MEIJI AGE

were at that time 486 Kazoku families and 406,209 Samurai families.

The country was in 1871 divided into three Fu[1] with the towns Tōkiō, Kiōto and Osaka. The Fu were again divided into seventy-two Ken.[2] The island of Ezo or Hokkaidō formed an exception, and was regarded as a colony, and also the island of Riūkiū which was governed by a king who paid homage to the imperial supremacy. But they were soon joined to a government district.[3]

At this period one reform followed another with astonishing rapidity. In 1870 the judicial system underwent reform: it was separated from the political administration. A new penal code was begun on the European model and was finished in 1880, and all legal affairs were administered in European fashion.

In 1871, also, a new system of coinage was introduced: the En (about two shillings) was the normal coin. A gold standard was only introduced after the victorious war with China. Europeans now founded banks and insurance societies in Japan.

The telegraph had been introduced in 1870; the next year the subterranean cable between Nagasaki

---

[1] Chief divisions.

[2] Government districts or departments.

[3] At the present time the country is divided into three Fu and forty-three Ken. Hokkaido, Formosa and Saghalien have a special government, as has the recently acquired Korea and the part of Manchuria ruled by Japan.

and Shanghai was laid. The railway between Tōkiō and Yokohama was opened in 1872, and other lines opening up the whole country soon followed. A postal system on the European model was instituted in 1871. In a few years there was a widely spread network of telegraphs. Compulsory education was made the law in 1872, and in 1873 the Gregorian calendar and the observance of Sunday were introduced.

Immediately after the breaking up of the feudal system, by the decree of June 17th, 1871, the former army of knights was disbanded, and replaced by an imperial army which in 1873 was to be joined by citizens and peasants. The formation, equipment and training of the imperial army followed the European model. French instructors were employed until 1877 and they were replaced later by German. Universal conscription was introduced in 1873. At that time the imperial army consisted of 6 divisions,[1] and each division had a peace footing of 7,000 men. An imperial navy was also founded at this time.

These reforms which were carried out by an absolute government were followed by the reform of the absolute government itself, and may be compared with the period of liberal-minded absolutism in European states when the people grew ripe for political independence and constitutional government.

But before this change occurred there was a fierce and widespread struggle to defend the reforms already made from the reaction that set in against them.

[1] It now consists of 18 divisions.

CHAPTER II

REACTION AGAINST THE NEW SYSTEM OF GOVERNMENT

IT can be easily understood that the activity of the reforming government, and the joyful acquiescence of the majority of the people, excited serious discontent in the class that had formerly played the chief part, and was now deprived of all its privileges. The Samurai found that in the general economic and industrial competition and progress they were outstripped by the citizens whom they had hitherto regarded with contempt. They were even deprived of what had formerly distinguished them outwardly from citizens and peasants, the right to wear two swords, by an edict of 1871. The money compensation they received was very small; in any case it bore no relation to their former way of living, and was soon spent. The only work they understood was that of fighting, and they had neither the capacity nor the desire for industrial or agricultural employments. Those, and they were the greater part, who received no office saw themselves face to face with poverty. The large party of opposition to the new system of government that was thus formed among the Samurai included many who, a short time before, had supported the imperial government against the Shōgunate. They had not foreseen that the restoration of the imperial power would result in the complete abolition of the feudal system, and the ruin of their class. As it was clear to most of them that there was very little chance of the restoration of feudal conditions, they placed their hopes on a foreign war by means of which they thought to win fame and esteem. And so the Samurai agitated for war with Korea.

They found support for their effort in that direction in General Saigō Takamori, a former Samurai of the Daimiō of Satsuma. He had won great distinction in the restoration of the imperial power, and held an important place at the imperial court. Many councillors of state of the various government departments supported their efforts, and in 1873 had very nearly succeeded in forcing their will, when Iwakura Tomomi, the Chancellor of the right, and the councillors of state, Okubo Toshimichi and Kido Takayoshi returned from a three years' tour in Europe, and declared that for the present, the government must under no circumstances enter into a foreign war; peace must be preserved in the land, in order to carry on the reforms already made and to introduce others. The Emperor shared the views of the reform and peace party. That fact so embittered the aristocratic leaders of the war party, Saigō Takamori, and the councillors Etō Shimpei and Itagaki Taisuke,

REACTION AGAINST THE NEW SYSTEM 209

that they resigned the imperial service. They now put themselves at the head of the opposition against the reforming government.

In 1874 a rebellion led by Etō Shimpei broke out in the Saga district and it took the government a month to quell it. It saw that danger to the country might ensue from this discontent, and that something must be done to divert the opposition's desire of fighting to other quarters. It therefore determined on an expedition to Formosa to subdue the savage tribes living in the south of the island. A legitimate political cause was forthcoming. A few years back Japanese merchants had been murdered there. Representations made at the time by Japan to the Chinese government to which Formosa was subordinate, were without result. Japan was therefore within its rights, if it now sought satisfaction on its own part.

In May, 1874, General Saigō Tsugumichi set out from Nagasaki to Formosa with 36,000 men, mostly Samurai, and in a few months succeeded in bringing the savage tribes of the island into subjection. But Japan was unable to annex a part of the island, as the Chinese government entered a protest against Japan's proceedings. Diplomatic negotiations ensued, and with the help of English arbitration it was decided that China should pay Japan an indemnity of £50,000

The enterprise, however, did not remove the discontent prevailing among the knights.

In 1876 rebellions again broke out. A large

number of Samurai collected together in the town of Kumamoto where there had been peculiar resistance to the introduction of European customs. In the night of October 24th-25th they attacked Major-General Taneda and numerous other officers of the garrison. Taneda and many of his comrades died. The prefect of the district was seriously wounded. The soldiers in the barracks were forced to surrender to the rebels. Revolts also occurred in Akitsuki and Hagi.

The next year, 1877, the rebellion that the former General Saigō Takamori had so long been preparing took place. He had belonged to the imperial party, and had supported the friendly policy of the government towards foreigners. But he possessed too much of the old spirit of chivalry, he was too much a child of feudal times, of too romantic a nature, not to find the policy of the imperial civil government too levelling. From patriotic motives he had eagerly supported the abolition of fiefs and the decree of June 17th, 1809, but he desired to preserve for the fatherland the chivalrous spirit of feudal times. He and many educated officers who gathered round him, considered it unworthy of a military state to be governed as now, solely by civil officials, and could not endure that so many brave Samurai should be reduced to a condition of absolute insignificance. Their aim was to replace this, in their opinion, weakly official system of government which they despised, by a strong, military rule, ready and able to pursue a glorious foreign policy, and to have no fear of entering on a war. They hoped that under such a government the Samurai would regain their rights.

The rebellion had been long preparing. With men of similar views like Major-General Kirino Toshiaki and Shinowara Kunimoto, Takamori had founded in his native Kagoshima the so-called private school. There the classical literature of China was studied and daily military exercises practised. The number of pupils gradually increased to 3,000.

In February, 1877, the discontent broke out into open deeds of violence against the government officials. This was against the will of Takamori who would have preferred to wait until his strength was more assured. But there was now no going back. With a force of 12,000 men he marched against the town of Kumamoto, where there was a strong imperial garrison that must be overcome before he could proceed to march against Tōkiō. The imperial Major-General Tani Motoki, the commander-in-chief of the garrison, made a brave resistance, and Saigō Takamori was forced to enter on a wearisome siege. He received support in money from the prefect of the district of Kagoshima, so that he was able to increase his army to 20,000 men. But soon Prince Arisugawa-no-miya marched against him with the whole imperial army.

A battle took place near Kumamoto on the hill of Tabaruzaka in which Saigō was defeated, and some of the best leaders of the rebel army like

Shinowara, fell. The siege of Kumamoto was raised soon after this defeat. When the rebels were defeated after severe fighting at several fortresses, Takamori and his faithful adherents returned to Kagoshima where they intrenched themselves on the hill of Schiroyama, situated near the town of Kagoshima. There on the morning of September 24th they were defeated by the imperial army after a final desperate struggle. Saigō Kirino, and other leaders committed suicide. The victory of the imperial troops put an end to the danger of rebellion by those opposed to the new system of government.

The tragic end of Takamori roused deep sympathy throughout the country both in friend and foe. A great personality died with him. He understood in a degree rarely seen, how to live and die for his great patriotic ideas, impossible to realize though they were. Not less than 40,000 men had taken up arms for him in the last war. His defeat cost the government a great expenditure of strength. They had placed in the field against him 58,000 men of whom 6,200 were killed and 9,500 wounded.

CHAPTER III

INTRODUCTION OF CONSTITUTIONAL GOVERNMENT

WE have already stated that a period of enlightenment followed the abolition of the feudal system in Japan, for which the absolute government was systematically responsible. By its means, European intellectual life took firm root in Japan. Simultaneously with the introduction of compulsory education and the extension of the system of elementary schools, numerous high schools were established in which European languages, especially English, were taught. English books were read, and Japanese students went every year to Europe and returned to their homes full of European ideas. And thus constitutional ideas and methods found favour, but more among educated persons like the higher officials than among the masses of the people.

The government made reforms before they were especially demanded or even understood by the people. In 1875 they instituted a Senate with regular sessions, composed of distinguished and capable men, and also an annual meeting of directors of districts. Both assemblies were of an advisory character. In 1879 district councils were instituted in each district, and they were responsible for an essential part of the financial administration and the imposition of taxes in their districts.

But gradually the new political ideas penetrated to the people themselves, and the demand for constitutional government became more insistent. Numerous petitions were presented to the senate concerning the revision of the commercial treaties, and the removal of the special tribunals of the foreign consulates. Different political parties were formed: 1. The Jiyūtō, the liberal party which demanded greater personal freedom. Its founder was the former councillor, Itugaki Taisuke, who had resigned with Saigō Takamori. 2. The Kaishintō, the progressive party, the less radical party which demanded national progress rather than the liberty of the individual. Its founder was the councillor, Okuma Shigenobu, who had also resigned, and later was to come forward as minister. 3. The Rikkenteiseitō, the constitutional imperial government party which held conservative views; it wanted a constitution but felt that the time for constitutional government had not yet arrived. That party had only existed for a short time. At the same time as this formation of parties, the press made great progress and the demands of public opinion were more definitely expressed.

These developments resulted in the following imperial decree of October, 1881:

"My family has been in uninterrupted possession of the government of this country for over 2,500 years. I have completely restored the imperial power which suffered diminution in the middle ages, and have re-united the whole Empire. It is my wish to give my people a system of constitutional government which shall be accepted and protected by my successors. The Senate and the assembly of directors of districts instituted in 1875 were a preparation for this. But the time is not yet ripe for the introduction of such a system. European civilization must first be more widely spread and more firmly rooted. But I promise that in the 23rd Meiji year, 1890, a parliament shall be opened. Let the officials and the people prepare for it."

In 1882 the Emperor sent the councillor, Itō Hirobumi, to Europe to study the different European constitutions. He returned to Japan in 1884, and a beginning was made to work out great government reforms.

In 1885 a thorough change was made in the official apparatus of the imperial central government. The Dajōkan, that had been restored in 1869 was abolished, and the central government was modelled on the European ministries. A President (Naikaku-Sōri-Daijin) was at the head of the following departments: 1. Home Office (Naimu-shō). 2. Foreign Office (Gaimu-shō). 3. The Treasury (Okura-shō). 4. War Office (Rikugun-shō). 5. The Admiralty (Kaigun-shō). 6. Department of Justice (Shihō-shō). 7. Board of Education (Mombu-shō). 8. Board of Agriculture and Trade (Nōshōmu-shō). 9. Board of Communications and Public Works (Teishin-shō).

The Senate instituted in 1875 was abolished, and the Emperor formed a privy council of men who had won distinction in the service of the State. The regular sittings of the district assembly also ceased, and it lay in future with the minister for Home Affairs to summon it for the purpose of advice in specially important matters.

In 1888 the administration of the communes underwent reform.

The proclamation of the new constitution which was awaited by the people with great anxiety was made on February 11th, 1889.

It instituted two chambers, the House of Lords and the House of Representatives of the people. The two chambers had the rights of regular sessions of imposing taxes, of legislation, of petition and of interpellation. The Emperor held the right of summoning, proroguing or dissolving both chambers, of setting aside their decisions or assisting them with the power of the law. This constitution still holds good.

The House of Lords, so ran the decree, was to consist of: 1. Princes of the imperial family over 20 years of age. 2. All princes and marquises over 25 years of age. 3. One fifth of the three other classes of nobles elected by themselves. The right of voting belonged only to those who had completed their 25th year. 4. 45 citizen delegates. The 15 richest men of each district elected a delegate, the age of 30 being the lowest both for elected and electors. The delegate was elected to serve for seven years. 5. Of a certain number of learned and capable men chosen by the Emperor according to his pleasure. The number of the members of the House of Lords was not to exceed 300.

The House of Representatives of the people, the decree stated, was to be directly elected. The electoral franchise was to be equal but not universal. Only those who paid 15[1] En in direct taxes and were over 25 years of age could vote. The members who numbered 300[2] were elected for 4 years.

Two important reforms were introduced before the beginning of the elections. A new legal constitution was decreed, February 18th, 1890, and a new civil code was published on February 21st.

The elections for the House of Representatives were held July, 1st-3rd, 1890. The result was favourable to the government. The Emperor opened both Chambers on November 29th, and thus in 1890 a new era again began for Japan.

---

[1] Lowered later to 10 En.
[2] Raised to 370 in 1890.

CHAPTER IV

RELATIONS OF JAPAN WITH RUSSIA AND WITH KOREA

WE have seen how at the end of the Tokugawa Shōgunate the Russians had penetrated as far as the northern frontier of Japan, and in spite of the opposition of the Shōgunate government had taken possession of a part of the islands of Saghalien and Kurile. Shortly before its fall the Shōgunate asserted its readiness to recognize the 50th parallel of north latitude as its boundary. But the Russian government did not agree. In 1875, however, the two powers came to an agreement by which Russia received the whole of Saghalien, and Japan the Kurile islands.

After the restoration of the imperial power in Japan, there was, as we have also seen, a strong agitation for war with Korea. The government was not in favour of it, considering the country not yet sufficiently prepared to risk the chances of so hazardous a foreign enterprise. But the Korean question was soon to become again acute. For the government of Korea which refused to open their ports to foreigners, and fired at French and American men of war, were too proud to receive a Japanese embassy, and made great encroachments on Japan. In 1895 a Japanese man of war sailed past the Korean island of Kōka, and was fired at from the battery of the island. An attack followed and the Japanese took the island. The success of the Japanese arms worked wonders. The Korean government contented themselves with entering into diplomatic relations with Japan, and concluding a commercial treaty by which the port of Fusan, and later those of Tschemulpo and Gensan, were open to Japan. The United States and the European governments made similar treaties with Korea.

Hitherto the government of Korea had been carried on by Tai-Wön-Kun, a man hostile to reform, for his son, King Ri-Ki, who was a minor. When he came of age and took over the reins of government in agreement with his wife, a member of the powerful aristocratic family, Min, he directed his efforts to obtain absolute independence, and to remove Tai-Wön-Kun's influence from all departments of the government. The contrast was the more acute since he sought to introduce reforms on the Japanese model. When for that purpose he invited some Japanese officers to visit the country, Tai-Wön-Kun was so exasperated that he collected an army of discontented soldiers, stormed the royal palace, and massacred the Japanese officers. The house of the Japanese embassy was burnt down, and the Japanese envoys only escaped with their lives, and fled to Nagasaki in an English ship.

But a change in the conduct of affairs at court took place when a Japanese man of war appeared at Tschemulpo and demanded satisfaction for the Japanese embassy. Fear of war with Japan shook Tai-Wön-Kun's determination, he left the palace and fled to Peking. The young king apologized to Japan and permitted her to place two companies of soldiers at Seoul. And the Korean government paid an indemnity of £50,000.

China now interfered, and also placed two companies of soldiers at Seoul, as Japan could not be permitted to strengthen her position in Korea. The rivalry between the Japanese and Chinese troops continually increased, and two parties corresponding to the rival nations were formed at the Korean court: the Jidaitō[1] which was re-actionary and leaned to China, and the Dokuritsutō[2] which held progressive views and leaned to Japan. In December, 1884, it came to open hostility. The Dokuritsutō attacked members of the Min family who had been disloyal to their friendship with Japan, and had joined with the Jidaitō party. Thereupon hostilities immediately broke out between the Japanese and Chinese garrisons which ended badly for the Japanese. The Japanese embassy was burnt down (1884).

But Japan made a protest, and the minister for Foreign Affairs went in person to Korea. The

---

[1] Ji=obedient, dai=great power *i.e.* China, to=party.
[2] *i.e.* independence.

Korean government made amends, promised to rebuild the Japanese embassy and to pay an indemnity.

In order also to come to a settlement with China, the Japanese ambassador Itō Hirobumi went to Tientsin where he entered into negociations with the Chinese Ambassador Li-Hung-Tschang. The Treaty of Tientsin was concluded between the two powers, 18th April, 1885. It enacted: 1. Recognition of the independence of Korea. 2. Withdrawal of the Chinese and Japanese troops. 3. Obligation of the two powers to come to an agreement together concerning all future action in Korea.

But the hostility between China and Japan in regard to Korea was not ended by that treaty, and the last article contained the germ of fresh conflicts.

CHAPTER V

THE CHINO-JAPANESE WAR

THE Chinese government had no intention of taking the Treaty of Tientsin seriously. They considered that their supremacy over Korea still held good, and continued to interfere considerably in the domestic affairs of the country.

When in April, 1894, the Tōkugatō[1] rebelled, and the Korean government could not put them down, China sent troops to Korea. That proceeding compelled Japan to do the same. Four thousand men were landed at Yen-Tschuan, not far from Seoul, on June 12th. The Chinese government informed Japan that their troops were not required, as China had already restored order. The Japanese government referred to the Treaty of Tientsin, and proposed that with the assistance of China, reforms should be carried out in Korea by which the country should be freed from the oppression of the nobles and from the extortions of corrupt officials. By that way alone could the improvement of the impoverished nation be assured.

[1] Tō=oriental, Gaku=learning, Tō=party.

THE CHINO-JAPANESE WAR

China refused the proposition without closer consideration, and sent more troops by sea to Asan (Gazan) in order to shut up the Japanese army in Seoul and destroy it.

Then a Japanese squadron of 8 ships sailed out and cruised about on the high seas before Asan in order to capture any further troops that China might send. On July 25th, it came up with two Chinese ships by the island of Pfhung-dō (Hōtō) near Asan. The Chinese fired the first shot; a fight took place that ended with the flight of the Chinese ships. Soon after the Japanese squadron again came up with two Chinese ships that had a large number of troops aboard. One of them immediately surrendered. The other that sailed under the British flag was summoned to surrender by Tōgō, the commander of the cruiser, Naniwa, and when she refused was fired at and destroyed. The English officers were saved, but 1200 Chinese troops who were on board were drowned.

Meanwhile the Japanese had landed more troops at Tschemulpo. They joined with the Japanese regiment at Seoul, and attacked the Chinese, who had remained at Asan waiting in vain for aid. A battle was fought on July 27th, at the little town of Seonghwan (Sei-kan) in which the Chinese were defeated.

The Korean government again deserted the Chinese cause for the side of the more powerful Japanese.

On August 1st, 1894, the Japanese government officially declared war on China, and were enthusiastically supported by the two Houses and the people in general. Party differences retired into the background, and the House of Representatives unanimously granted the necessary funds.

On August 8th, the Japanese marched into Seoul unopposed, and were received in friendly fashion by the Korean Government which declared its readiness to make the reforms demanded by Japan.

As the Japanese fleet made it impossible for the Chinese to effect a landing at Asan, they had landed troops in the north of Korea at the mouth of the river Taidong, and occupied the fortress of Phyöng-yang which was situated in its neighbourhood. Thither also the troops retreated after their defeat at Sŏng-hwan. The garrison of Phyöng-yang was increased therefore to 50,000 men. The Japanese sent a part of their force against the fortress, under the command of Lieutenant-General Nozu, who took it by storm on September 15th.

Two days later, a naval battle took place near the island of Hai-yang in the Korean bay of the Yellow Sea. The Japanese fleet consisted of 12 ships, and was under the command of Itō Yukō, the Chinese fleet numbering 12 men of war and 5 torpedo boats. The battle ended with the entire defeat of the Chinese who lost five ships.

The chief military encampment which had been hitherto at Tōkiō was moved on September 15th to the west, to Hiroshima, so as to be nearer the seat of war.

Before the taking of the fortress of Phyöng-yang, Field-Marshal Yamagata Aritomo with the fifth and third divisions, had crossed the lower course of the Yalu, the river that formed the boundary between Korea and Manchuria, and invaded Manchuria. The Chinese had a fortress, Kiu-lien-cheng, (Kiū-ren-jō) on the Manchurian bank of the Yalu, and a force of 25,000 men. When on October 26th, the Japanese began the attack, the whole of the Chinese garrison turned tail and fled. Sixty-six cannon, more than 3,000 guns and large military stores, fell into the hands of the Japanese.

After the capture of that fortress the second Japanese army, consisting of the 1st and 2nd divisions under Field-Marshal Oyama Iwao landed on the east coast of the Liantung peninsula at the mouth of the river Hwa-Yen (Ka-en-kō), not far from Port Arthur (Rio-jun-Kō). They immediately attacked the fortified town of Kintschou, took it on November 6th, and so threw open the road to Port Arthur. On November 21st, they attacked that fortress but were repulsed. In the night, however, the Chinese fled, and when the Japanese renewed the attack next day, they found no resistance. Thus the southern peninsula of Liangtung fell into the hands of the 2nd Japanese army which now divided into two parts. The principal division, under Oyama, embarked for the Shantung peninsula, the other, under the command of Lieutenant-General Yamaji marched north in order to join the 1st army which had meanwhile penetrated farther into Manchuria.

The next proceeding of the northern army (1st army) was to attack the fortress of Kaiping in the north of the Liantung peninsula, and they took it by storm on January 10th, 1895.

The passage of the larger part of the 2nd army to the Shantung peninsula was accomplished under the protection of the whole of the Japanese fleet of men of war. The troops were landed, January 20th-25th. They immediately proceeded to attack the fortress of Wei-hai-wei. The whole of the Chinese war fleet, about 30 men of war, was lying in the harbour. They had barricaded themselves there, and despite their numerical superiority, made no attempt to prevent the passage of the Japanese southern army. During the attack of the land force on the fortress, the Japanese fleet blockaded the harbour. The south-east fort fell on January 30th, and on February 2nd, the Japanese were masters of all the fortifications situated on the mainland. During the battle they had several times attacked the Chinese fleet with torpedo boats, in consequence of which they suffered some losses, but destroyed four of the enemy's men of war. The Japanese fleet and land force now combined in common attacks on the enemy's ships and island forts, and by February 12th, Admiral Ting, Commander of the Chinese fleet, was compelled to enter into negotiations. The deed of capitulation was signed on February 14th. Ting killed himself before the surrender. The other ten men of war, and a garrison of 5,134 men and 183 officers fell into the hands of the Japanese. The prisoners had to surrender their arms, and were then set at liberty.

While the southern army had had so brilliant a

success, the northern army had also been victorious General Nozu had replaced Yamagata who had been forced to resign through illness. On March 4th, Nozu had taken the town of Niu-tschwang after severe fighting in the streets, and then crossed the Liau-ho (Riō-ka) with the whole of the northern army. The town of Tien-tschwang-tai (Den-shō-dai) was soon taken, and then there were no troops to prevent the further invasion of the Chinese empire by the Japanese. And so the large empire of China was compelled to make overtures of peace to little Japan.

Japan had won the admiration of the whole world by its deeds of arms. The new era had produced fine fruit. It was evident that the Japanese nation understood how to assimilate the technical inventions and the military drill of Europe and to employ it themselves. But they did not owe their splendid success to that alone. Their character, their long inherited warlike spirit, was what chiefly evoked praise in this war. It is rightly expressed by Professor Nitobe in his " Bushidō:" " It has been said that Japan owed her success in her last war with China to Murata rifles and Krupp guns, to her adoption of modern systems of education—but those are only half-truths. The most perfect guns and cannon do not shoot of themselves. The modern system of education does not make a hero out of a coward. No! What won the battles on the Yalu, in Korea and in Manchuria were the spirits of our ancestors who guided our hands and who were enthroned in our hearts. They are not dead, the spirits of our warlike forefathers. For those who have eyes to see, they are clearly visible."

On March 19th China sent its celebrated diplomatist, Li-Hung-Tschang, with his son to Japan. The negociations for peace took place in Shimonoseki (or Bakan). Japan was represented by the Prime Minister, Itō Hirobumi, and Mutsu Munemitsu, Minister of Foreign affairs. Peace was concluded on April 17th.

The terms of the Peace of Shimonoseki were as follows:

1. China recognised the absolute independence of Korea.
2. The following places were to be ceded to Japan.
   a. The Lian-Tung peninsula.
   b. The island of Formosa (or Taiwan) and the small islands thereto belonging.
   c. The island of Hōkotō.
3. China to pay Japan a war indemnity of two hundred million taels.
4. China to open to Japanese trade in addition to the places already accessible Schaschi in Hupet, Tschung-King in Szet-schnan, Sutschou in Kiangsu and Hang-tschow in Tschekiang.
5. As guarantee for the execution of the Treaty, China to cede the fortress of Wei-hai-wei to Japan which was to be evacuated by Japan after payment of the indemnity and fulfilment of all the other conditions.

But Russia objected to these terms. She saw obstacles to her own plans in the cession of the peninsula of Lian-tung to Japan. She had already thoughts of acquiring Port Arthur for her maritime operations. Russia was supported at Tōkiō by German and French diplomacy. Those powers founded their objection on the fact that the garrison of Lian-tung by Japan would threaten peace in the far east. There was nothing left for Japan except to yield, and full of bitter anger she saw herself deprived of the reward for which she had so bravely fought and which she so well deserved. Itō Hirobumi was forced to sign the treaty on November 8th, 1895, giving up Lian-tung to China for an increase of the war indemnity by 30 million taels.

The germ of the Russo-Japanese war lay in this treaty. For Japan had no idea of permanently submitting to Russia's desire of expansion, and waited for the time when she could meet that great power on terms of military equality.

The possession of the island of Formosa caused some fighting. The Chinese population of Formosa rebelled under the leadership of the Chinese Su-Yung-Fu, the well-known head of the "Black Flag," a party in China which had made so stubborn a resistance to the invasion of Cochin China by the French. Japan sent a large army to Formosa under the command of Prince Kitashirakawa-no-miya The rebellion was entirely put down by the middle of December.

CHAPTER VI

THE REVISION OF THE COMMERCIAL TREATIES

As we have seen, the first commercial treaties were concluded by the Shōgunate government in 1858. At a period of domestic unrest, and of a weak foreign policy, it had granted great advantages to foreign powers at the expense of the Japanese Empire. The duty which Japan laid on foreign imports was very low. It was, moreover, especially derogatory and offensive to Japan that all foreigners were subject not to the Japanese courts of justice but to special consular courts of their own. Japan in that matter was treated like an uncivilized nation, and the circumstance often led to great injustice. The treaties of 1858 were made worse for Japan in the following years, for numerous attacks were made on the foreigners, and in compensation Japan had to make further concessions to the foreign powers. It was natural that the advancement of civilization in the Japanese nation should cause a demand for the revision of the existing treaties.

In 1878, Terajima Munenori, minister for foreign affairs, had approached England with a proposal of

THE COMMERCIAL TREATIES

revision, which England refused. In 1882 Japan renewed her proposals, and entered into negotiations with all the foreign powers who showed themselves willing to make a few concessions. England proposed to abolish the consular courts, and to establish mixed courts, formed of both Japanese and foreign judges. But the announcement of these proposals raised a storm of opposition among the Japanese people. Okuma Shigenobu, the foreign minister who desired to accede to the English compromise of mixed courts was violently attacked, and in 1889 lost his right leg through a bomb thrown by a patriot. The negociations therefore fell through.

It was not till August 27th, 1894, due to the impression produced by the glorious successes of the Japanese arms in China, that the foreign minister, Mutsu Munemitsu was able to conclude a new commercial treaty with England which fulfilled the Japanese requirements. Treaties with the other powers on a similar basis were soon concluded; with Germany, April 4th, 1896.

These commercial treaties abolished the consular courts, introduced a higher protection tariff for Japan, opened the whole country to foreigners, and set some new ports free for trade with foreign powers. But the qualification still held that foreigners might only acquire a small amount of landed property, a qualification that was not removed until 1910.

CHAPTER VII

THE CHINESE TROUBLES

THE war between Japan and China made the Eastern question and Eastern affairs a focus of interest in Europe, and in the policy of the Great Powers. Russia, in particular, was making every effort to secure a firm position on the coasts of Eastern Asia. With a vast expenditure of strength she completed the Trans-Siberian railway. But the other Great Powers also tried to secure influence in the far east. In November, 1897, Germany occupied the port of Kiau-Tshou, on the south coast of the peninsula of Shantung, in order to have a footing for her fleet, and on March 6th, 1898, made an agreement with the Chinese government by which the Bay of Kiau-Tshou with the adjacent territory was leased to the German Empire for 99 years. During this time Russia had also been negociating with the Chinese government, and on March 27th, 1898, concluded with China a deed of conveyance for 25 years for the south-west portion of the peninsula of Liantung with Port Arthur. The treaty also allowed Russia to continue the Trans-Siberian railway through

Manchuria to Niu-Tschwang and the ports of Port Arthur and Ta-lien-wan (Dairen). On April 2nd, 1898, England received Wei-hai-wei on condition that she would cede it to China when Port Arthur again became Chinese. England took possession of the port and the islands belonging to it and about 460 square miles of the adjacent mainland. France would not be left out, and in the same month and year obtained a deed of conveyance for 99 years for the Bay of Kwan-tshou on the coast of the province of Canton. The next year she received in addition the island of Tung-shan and some smaller islands. She acquired in all about 521 square miles.

These great sacrifices to which China had to consent roused in the nation great indignation which was directed against all foreigners. The imperial family did nothing to suppress the movement, indeed, it rather assisted in stirring up hatred of the foreigner. The exasperation was keenest in the north, in the neighbourhood of Tientsin and Peking. That district was the seat of the so-called Boxer rebellion of 1900.

A plot was made against the foreigners, the purpose of which was a rebellion. The members of the conspiracy called themselves Giwadan, i.e. peace and patriotic union. The league began public action at the commencement of 1900. Many foreigners, among them Japanese, soon fell victims. The native Christians were cruelly persecuted. The rebels destroyed the railways in every direction. In May the German Ambassador and a secretary of the

Japanese embassy were murdered. The embassies of the Foreign Powers at Peking were besieged. The English admiral, Sir Edward Seymour, marched to their assistance with an army composed of European, American and Japanese troops, but had to turn back without doing anything, (10th-26th June). The Chinese government secretly supported the rebels. They openly opposed the foreign auxiliary troops, e.g. at the defence of the fort of Taku and of Tientsin. The Japanese played an important part in the storming, of the fort of Taku (June 17th) by the foreign powers and in the fighting at Tientsin (July 14th). Japan sent the 5th division under the command of Lieutenant-General Yamaguchi to the seat of war, 6th July. The timely release of the embassies shut up in Peking is mainly due to the speedy intervention of this large contingent of Japanese troops (15th August.)

By the peace signed on December 22nd, 1901, China had to pay the Foreign Powers 400,000,000 taels war indemnity.

The importance of this outbreak against the foreigners was that it afforded Russia an opportunity to secure a firm military footing in Manchuria. She had been striving with all her force to carry out the construction of the Manchurian railway, had made expensive military settlements, and under pretext of protecting the railway from Chinese attacks, had located there 200,000 men. Thus Manchuria, and also the much disputed peninsula of Liantung, were entirely under the military power of Russia. Russia had reaped advantages to herself out of this to her not unwelcome rebellion as she had out of the Chino-Japanese war. But Japan stood in the way of the further execution of her plan of securing a great position in the far east.

CHAPTER VIII

THE RUSSO-JAPANESE WAR

THE tension between Russia and Japan had existed ever since Russia's interference in the conditions of the Peace of Shimonoseki between Japan and China. The Japanese had to look on while Russia appropriated the booty for which they had so bravely fought. Japan had followed with great anxiety the expansion of the Russian power during the Boxer rebellion. It was to be feared that Korea, where already so much Japanese blood had been spilled and with which Japan was so closely bound through its history, would fall a prey to the Russian lust of conquest. The question, in whose possession that district was to be in the future, was one of life and death to Japan. If Russia became lord of the Sea of Japan, then Japan must for ever abandon the hope of winning a position of equality among the great powers.

Japan now came to an understanding with England who looked on at the Russian expansion with great misgiving. In February, 1902, the two powers concluded a treaty in which they bound themselves to stand together for the independence of China and Korea. The treaty further stipulated that if either of the powers was attacked by two great powers the other should come to its assistance with all its military forces. It was hoped by this means to frighten Russia from making further encroachments.

Supported by her powerful ally, the Japanese government entered into negociations with Russia. It demanded the withdrawal of the troops from Manchuria. But Russia had not the smallest intention of abandoning the further prosecution of her policy; she sought to delay the negociations as long as possible in order to strengthen and reinforce her troops in Manchuria. The counter-proposals delivered at last on October 3rd, 1903, resembled a challenge. The essential points were: both powers to maintain the independence and integrity of Korea; Russia would recognise Japan's interests in Korea. Japan must undertake to place no fortifications on the Korean road, and must acknowledge that Manchuria lay outside its sphere of interest. The position Russia would hold with regard to Manchuria was not mentioned.

That Russia should have staked so much on her enterprises in the far east and that she should seek to bring about so dangerous a war is easily understood. Great interests for the empire of the Czar were here at stake. The success of her plans in the far east meant an enormous increase of power for Russia. The acquisition of Manchuria with excellent ports both for war and commerce which were already partly provided with expensive works, and the railway connected with the European continent would have made Russia the strongest power in the east. The mastery of the Eastern Sea would have given her the prospect of enormous economic profit. It would have meant only one road for trade from the Manchurian trading ports on the Yellow Sea to the Eastern Sea. Her great Asiatic possessions would have been objects of immense value. Just as for Japan this question was one of life and death, on it depended for Russia her future position in the world. The value of such advantages for the political power and economic life of the empire of the Czar made it worth while to venture on a dangerous war.

Even after the unacceptable proposals made by Russia on October 3rd, the Japanese government continued the negociations, but as was to be expected without success. On February 6th, 1904, a final note was sent to the government at St. Petersburg, breaking off the negociations, and declaring that Japan would now proceed as was necessary for the protection of her threatened position, and the safety of her rights and interests. Kurino, the Japanese ambassador at St. Petersburg, was recalled on February 8th. The official declaration of war followed on February 10th.

The Japanese fleet had already on February 6th, sailed under the command of Vice-Admiral Tōgō Heihachirō from the port of Sasebo to the south-west coast of Korea. Arrived there, Rear-Admiral Uriu separated from it with a division of cruisers in order to take possession of Tschemulpo where two Russian ships were lying. The chief division under Tōgō went on to Port Arthur.

The greater part of the Port Arthur Russian fleet lay in the outer roadstead, for the inner harbour was not sufficiently ready. It did not expect to be attacked and had taken no precautions. In the nights 8th to 9th February, the Japanese made a successful torpedo attack by which two big Russian ironclads and a cruiser were damaged.

Rear-Admiral Uriu was also successful at Tschemulpo. In the night 8th to 9th February he secretly landed two regiments in the neighbourhood of the port which marched immediately to the capital, Seoul. The next day he forced the Russian cruisers to a fight, and they fled back into the harbour. The Russian commander sank both ships. The Japanese took possession of Tschemulpo where it was intended to land the first Japanese army.

Admiral Tōgō tried to blockade the harbour of Port Arthur by sinking old steamships, bombarded it, made torpedo attacks on it, and laid mines. But these attempts did not bring the desired result. The Russian admiral Stark was recalled, and Admiral Makarov appointed Commander-in-chief at Port Arthur. On the morning of April 13th there was a fight between Russian and Japanese torpedo boats. Admiral Makarov sent out the whole of his fleet. But when he eame in sight of the Japanese fleet drawn up for the attack, and recognised their superiority, he gave the order to retreat. His flagship Petropavlovsk struck a mine, and immediately sank. Makarov and all his crew were killed. A second ironclad was also considerably damaged by a mine during the retreat. Later Tōgō succeeded in completely blockading the harbour.

In February the Russian cruisers lying at Vladivostock sailed over to the coast of Japan and destroyed a Japanese merchant vessel. In return Admiral Kamimura went over to Vladivostock with some cruisers, and bombarded it on March 6th. Not much was thereby gained, and he soon departed. In the further course of the war Vladivostock played no essential part.

Immediately after the victory at Tschemulpo the 12th division embarked at Nagasaki and on February 17th landed at Tschemulpo, and at once marched to Seoul. The Emperor of Korea made an alliance with the Japanese and granted them the right of making what use they pleased of Korea so long as the war lasted. More troops were landed at Tschemulpo and at Tshinampo, situated to the north of Tschemulpo. By the end of April the Japanese had three divisions on the Yalu, the river dividing Korea from Manchuria. They formed the first Japanese army. General Kuroki was in command.

On February 20th, Kuropatkin, formerly minister of war, took over the command of the Russian troops. He arrived on March 27th, at Liau-yang, the head-quarters of the Russian army in Manchuria. General Stössel was governor of Port Arthur.

The Russians, as the Japanese had been doing, pushed on troops to the Yalu. There, on the morning of May 1st, a fierce battle was fought which ended in the defeat and retreat of the Russians. Their losses were: 30 officers and 581 men killed; 31 officers and 1,022 men wounded; 2 officers and 524 men taken prisoner by the Japanese. The Japanese losses were: 5 officers and 180 men killed; 25 officers and 690 men wounded. Military supplies, 21 cannon and 8 machine guns fell into the hands of the victors.

The first victory over a well equipped modern European army in the open field raised the courage of the Japanese.

Soon after the battle of the Yalu, Japanese troops were landed at Pi-Asje-wo, a short distance from Port Arthur. On May 5th the 1st, 3rd and 4th divisions, and the 1st field artillery brigade disembarked there. Their aim was to act in concert with the Japanese fleet against Port Arthur. The Russians had assembled about 27,000 men in the town of Kin-Tshou for the protection of Port Arthur. The Japanese directed a fierce artillery fire against it, stormed it on May 25th and took it after severe fighting. Sixty-eight cannon and 10 machine guns came into their possession. The Russians retired in the direction of Port Arthur. On May 28th the Japanese pushed forward a division to the hill of Hou-na-kwan-ling, and therefore General Stössel retreated to Port Arthur.

By the Czar's orders Kuropatkin sent a division of

the Manchurian army to the assistance of the hard pressed fortress. To prevent it joining with the garrison of Port Arthur, the Japanese sent the 4th division, the first field artillery brigade, and later the 3rd division under the command of General Oku, by forced marches to the north. They came up with the Russian auxiliary force at Toku-ri-ji. A fierce battle ensued in which the Japanese were again the victors. The Russians suffered great losses and retreated to the chief army at Liau-yang. General Oku went after them in hot pursuit. Since their departure from Kin-Tshou, his troops formed the second Japanese army which henceforth acted independently against the Manchurian army.

The troops that had remained at Port Arthur under General Nogi which now formed the third Japanese army, consisted of the 1st and 11th divisions, and was soon augmented by the 9th division, the 1st and 4th reserve brigade, the 2nd field artillery brigade and a regiment of heavy artillery. At the end of June they concentrated their energy on the siege of Port Arthur.

A fourth Japanese army was formed of the rest of the troops that had left their native land, under the command of General Nozu. Immediately on landing at Ta-ko-shan, it marched north and took part in the operations against the Manchurian army which continued to hold the defensive at Liau-yang. Field-Marshal Oyama was commander-in-chief of the three united Japanese armies.

The three armies (I, II, IV,) began the attack on

Liau-yang from different sides on August 30th. The victory was again to the Japanese. General Kuropatkin saved the greater part of his army by a cautious retreat for which he deserves every praise. The Japanese marched into Liau-yang on September 7th. The number of killed and wounded on the Russian side was 16,000, on the Japanese 17,000. The latter gained a large amount of booty.

The Russians had retreated in the direction of Mukden, and took up a position to the south of the river Hun-ho. The Japanese pursued them and intrenched themselves opposite in the plain of San-ho. A battle was begun on October 9th which lasted until October 18th. After a terrible struggle, Oyama and his three armies were victorious. The Russians lost 800 officers and 45,000 men, and the Japanese had 15,878 killed and wounded together. After this great defeat the Russians retreated to Mukden.

Meanwhile the third Japanese army was spending all its strength on the siege of Port Arthur. At the first general attack on August 19th, the western fort, Banriū, was taken, at the second on September 19th, the forts of Stössel and Kuropatkin fell into their hands, and the third, on October 26th, gave them the fort, Keikan-San, on the east.

Their bold proceedings at Port Arthur led to great losses on the Japanese side. But they could not avoid the sacrifice. For, as we shall see, Russia's Atlantic fleet was on the way, and everything depended on the taking of Port Arthur before its arrival, so that the Japanese sea-power should have the upper hand.

Admiral Tōgō encouraged the land forces to do their utmost.

After the third general attack, the Japanese succeeded in gaining possession of a hill about 600 feet high, whence the Russian ships that lay in the admirable harbour safe from Japanese attacks, could be carefully watched. The Japanese brought up heavy artillery behind the hill, and shooting under cover, on November 30th, destroyed the whole of the Russian Port Arthur fleet.

The fourth general attack was made on December 26th when some important forts were taken. These successes of the Japanese forced General Stössel to capitulate. In recognition of their courage, the victors allowed the Russian officers to keep their swords, and to return to their native land.

The fortress was surrendered on January 1st, 1905. The Japanese came into possession of 641 prisoners, 528 cannon, 206,734 artillery shells, 36,598 rifles, 5,450,240 bullets, etc. But these great military stores counted little beside the importance of the possession of the harbour for the further prosecution of the naval war which through the despatch of Russia's Atlantic fleet to the seat of war, entered on a new phase.

After the battle in the plain of San-ho, the opposing forces consisted of 300,000 Russians and 260,000 Japanese. The Japanese were reinforced by the third army which after the taking of Port Arthur marched north against the Manchurian army. The

THE RUSSO-JAPANESE WAR 245

four Japanese armies united on March 1st, 1905, in storming Mukden. The battle, which is one of the most splendid in the world's history, lasted for 10 days, and was fought on both sides with unexampled self-sacrifice and stubbornness. 120,000 Russians fell in the fight, and 40,000 were taken prisoner. The Japanese who fell numbered 41,222. On March 10th, the Japanese marched into Mukden in triumph.

The greater part of the Russian Atlantic fleet under command of Admiral Rovjestensky left Libau on October 12th, 1904, for the seat of war in order to go to the assistance of Port Arthur. The capture of the fortress and the destruction of the fleet here struck a severe blow at this maritime enterprise, but did not decide its fate. It was possible for the Russian squadron to destroy the Japanese fleet which equalled theirs in number, or at least to reach Vladiwostok and thence to conduct surprise attacks on the Japanese coast, and endanger the transports of Japan on their way to the seat of war.

Part of the Russian fleet took the route round the Cape of Good Hope, and another part that through the Mediterranean. At the request of Admiral Rovjestensky, the Czar despatched the rest of the Atlantic fleet on February 5th, and it took the shorter Mediterranean route. The Russian squadrons met off the coast of Annan, and proceeded together to the north. The Japanese fleet had secretly taken up its position in the straits of Korea. Vladivostok could be reached by three routes: through the straits of Korea, through the straits of Tsugaru between the islands of Hontō and Ezo, and through the straits of Sōya, between the islands of Ezo and Saghalien. It was impossible for the Japanese navy to defend all three straits at one time, for they would not when divided have been equal to the Russian fleet. Tōgō reckoned that the enemy, through the strictest secrecy regarding the Japanese position, would take the nearest route through the straits of Korea. His assumption was correct. The Russians had no knowledge of the whereabouts of the Japanese fleet, and proceeded up the straits of Korea.

At 5 a.m. in the morning of May 27th, one of the guardships posted in the south, sent the following message to Admiral Tōgō by wireless telegraphy: "The enemy's squadron has been sighted at point No. 203. The enemy is apparently steering towards the eastern passage." Between 10 and 11 o'clock the cruiser squadron under Vice-Admiral Kataoka, the division under Rear-Admiral Tōgō Masaji, and the division under Rear-Admiral Dewa came into touch with the enemy between the islands of Iki and Tsushoma. They did not answer their fire and contented themselves by telegraphing every moment all details of the enemy's position to Admiral Tōgō. Thus Tōgō knew before he came in sight of the enemy's fleet that its fighting line consisted of the whole strength of the second and third Atlantic squadron which were accompanied by about seven special service ships, that the ships were formed in two fore and aft lines, that the chief strength was at the head of the right line and the service ships were at the end, and that the whole armada was steering north-east at a speed of about 12 knots. Tōgō could now make plans in accordance, and give his orders. The battle was begun at 2 o'clock by the Japanese, near Okinoshima. Tōgō signalled to all ships in sight the following message: "The existence of the Empire depends on this battle. Japan expects this day the courage and energy of every officer and every man in the fleet." Tōgō with the chief strength, the Dewa and Uriu divisions, went against the head of the left column; the cruiser squadron and the Tōgō (Masaji) squadron steered south and attacked the enemy in the rear. The Russian fleet fell into disorder, the two columns came to blows, and sought in vain to free themselves and escape from the net prepared for them by the Japanese. The battle lasted till sunset. At 20 minutes past seven Tōgō ordered his fleet to assemble at the island of Ullong. The issue of the fight was decidedly favourable to the Japanese. A large number of the finest Russian ships were sunk, the rest were almost without exception badly damaged. The Japanese suffered no losses. In the night the destroyers and torpedo boats began to be active, and showed great boldness; some of them approached so close to the Russian ships that the later could not shoot at them. The Japanese did an enormous amount of damage, but themselves only lost 3 torpedo-vessels. The next morning (May 28th) the Japanese fleet with its whole strength continued the work of destruction. At half-past 10 the Russian fleet was entirely surrounded at a point 18 nautical miles south of Takenoshima. Soon after the Japanese opened fire, Rear-Admiral Nebugatov declared the surrender of the 4 ships under his command. The battle against the rest continued until noon. Then the destroyer Bjedovie, on board which was Admiral Rovjestensky and his staff, hoisted the white flag. Of the whole Russian fleet which had consisted of 38 ships, only two returned to Vladivostok. Of the rest, 23 were sunk, 7 were captured and 6 disarmed at Shanghai. The Japanese lost only the 3 torpedo-boats.

This brilliant and remarkable naval victory[1] signified not only the end of the Russian fleet, but also the end of the severe and momentous struggle.

In spite of her heavy losses and of the revolution that had taken place at home during the war, the great Russian empire was not by a long way at the end of her power. It was not difficult for Russia quickly to reinforce and increase her Manchurian army, and in spite of the defeats she had suffered, to make a successful stand against victorious but exhausted Japan. But the terrible impression of the last Japanese naval victory deprived Russia of courage to prosecute the war farther and inclined her to consider proposals for peace.

Soon after the naval battle in the Sea of Japan, Mr. Roosevelt, President of the United States, on June 9th, 1905, invited Japan and Russia to negociate

[1] Called in Japan "Naval battle in the Sea of Japan," in Europe "the battle of Tsushima."

conditions of peace. The proposal was accepted by both nations. Japan appointed as her plenipotentiaries Ko-Mura Jutarō, minister for foreign affairs, and Takahira Kogorō, her ambassador to the United States. Russia sent Witte a former minister of finance, and Rosen, formerly ambassador to Japan, to the peace conference. The plenipotentiaries met at Portsmouth, Maine, in the United States, on August 9th, 1905, and after 11 meetings peace was signed on August 29th.

The most important articles of the Peace of Portsmouth are :

Russia recognises that from the political, military and administrative standpoints, Japan's interests in Korea are supreme, and undertakes not to oppose the measures of government, protection and control which Japan deems necessary in agreement with the Korean government to take (Art 2).

Both powers shall withdraw their troops from Manchuria which is to remain Chinese (Art. 3).

The Russian rights of rental of Port Arthur, Talien, and the abutting land and sea to be surrendered entirely to Japan (Art 4).

The Manchurian railway to be divided between Russia and Japan at Kuang-Tscheng-Tse. Both divisions to be used only in the interests of trade and industry; Russia keeps all the rights acquired for the construction of the railway through her stipulations with China (Art. 6).

Russia and Japan are bound to join their roads at Kuang-Tscheng-Tse (Art. 7).

Russia relinquishes the southern part of Saghalien to the 50th degree of latitude to Japan (Art. 8).

The Japanese nation regarded the peace, considering their achievement, as extremely unfavourable. They were especially disappointed at the lack of any war indemnity. The angry excitement in Tōkiō rose so high that the police buildings were burnt down.

But although the peace was a disappointment to the victorious nation, it meant a great extension of Japanese power and influence. The Japanese gained a territory for their civilization and their economic activities measuring two-thirds of the extent of their empire hitherto. A stream of Japanese emigrants at once poured into the new territory; by May 1910 there were 157,000 Japanese in Korea. Immediately after the conclusion of peace, Japan appointed a Resident-General to govern the country, and he ruled it actually his own way, though formally in the name of the Emperor of Korea. Attempts on the part of Korea to restore the independence of the empire were unsuccessful and at the moment of concluding this history,[1] the Japanese can, by the treaty concluded with Russia in June, 1910, incorporate the Korean empire with their own without any opposition from the Powers.

---

[1] August 29, 1910.

INDEX

A

Abe Masahiro, 178, 179
Abe-no-Hirafu, the general, 41
Abe-no-Nakamaro, the scholar, 49
Abe-no-Yoritoki, 67
Abe Tadaaki, 165
Achiki, 21
Achino-mi, 21
Adams, William, 157
Aga-no-gawa, the river, 197
Ainus, the, 1, 2, 12, 13, 41, 51
Aizu, town of, 141, 197
Akamatsu family, the 112
Akamatsu Norimura, 97, 102, 103
Akechi Mitsuhide, 132
Akitsuki, 210
Alexander the Great, 31
Amako family, 122
Amakusa, island of, 162, 163
Amakuwa (Makao), 157
Amaterasu-Omikami, temple of, 147
Amaterasu-Omikami, the Sun-goddess, 7, 8, 26
Ancestor-worship, 27
Ando Nobumasa, 183
Anegawa, the, 130
Annan, 157, 245
Antoku-Tennō, 81st Emperor, 79, 80, 81
Aoka Todasuke, 170
Arai Hakuseki, 169
Arima, 157
Arisugawa-no-miya Taruhito, prince, 194, 195, 196, 211
Asan (Gazan), 223, 224
Asakura family, the, 130
Asai family, the, 130
Ashikaga family, the, 97, 116, 118, 120, 125, 129, 131
Ashikaga Takauji, 98, 102, 103, 104, 105, 106
Ashikaga Yoshiaki, 119, 130, 131
Ashikaga Yoshiharu, 119
Ashikaga Yoshihide, 119
Ashikaga Yoshitane, 119
Atlantic Ocean, 158
Atsuchi, castle of, 133
Awa, province of, 121

B

Bakan, fort of, 185
Bakan straits, 185
Bälz, 1
Bathu, 91
Benkei, 87
Biwa, lake of, 42
Boxer rebellion, 233, 234, 236
Buddhism, 25, 26, 27, 28, 29, 31, 48, 53, 93, 94, 125, 131, 132, 163
Bushidō, 151, 152, 153, 154, 203, 227

C

Cape of Good Hope, 157, 245
Chamberlain, 1
Chang-an, capital of Chinese Empire, 51
Chikamatsu Monzaimon, the dramatist, 166
China, 18, 23, 30, 31, 33, 41, 42, 45, 46, 49, 53, 65, 91, 117, 124, 125, 126, 137, 138, 139, 159, 209, 211, 220, 221, 223, 227, 228, 229, 232, 233, 236, 237
Chinese, language of the, 2
Chin-han (Shinkan), 17
Chōsen (or Chōsun) dynasty, 124
Chōsun (Chōsen), state of, 17
Chōsokabe Motochika, 122, 135
Chūai-Tennō, 14th Emperor, 16
Chūkiō-Tennō, 85th Emperor, 89, 90
Cochin China, 229
Confucius, bible of, 21
Confucius, teaching of, 165, 166

INDEX

D

Daigagu-ji, temple of, 97
Daigo-Tennō, 60th Emperor, 59, 60, 64, 65
Dan-no-ura Sea, 81
Date Masamune, 122, 158
Dewa, province of, 167
Dōkiō, Buddhist priest, 48, 49
Donchō of Korea, Buddhist priest, 32
Dsingiskhan, 91
Dutch, the, 156, 157, 164, 171, 176

E

Echigo, province of, 121, 197
Edo, 141
Emishi, 85
England, 179, 182, 230, 231, 233, 236
Enomoto Takeaki, 198
Enriakuji, temple of, 73, 130
Eskimos, the, 2
Etō Shimpei, 208, 209
Ezo (Hokkaidō), island of, 1, 176, 177, 179, 198, 205, 246

F

Finns, language of the, 2
Formosa (Taiwan), 137, 159, 160, 209, 228, 229
France, 182, 233
Fujiwara family, the 43, 52, 57, 58, 59, 61, 63, 64, 65, 67, 71, 72, 73, 76, 86, 89, 93, 111, 135, 188
Fujiwara Fubito, 44
Fujiwara Hidesato, 63
Fujiwara Ietaka, the poet, 93
Fujiwara Kanera, the poet, 117
Fujiwara Michinaga, 64, 65
Fujiwara Narichika, 78
Fujiwara Nobuzane, the painter, 95
Fujiwara Shūnzei, the poet, 93
Fujiwara Sumitomo, 62, 63
Fujiwara Tadahira, 62
Fujiwara Takaie, 66
Fujiwara Teika, the poet, 93
Fushimi-Tennō, 92nd Emperor, 96
Fushimi, town of, 135
Fusan, port of, 219

G

Gemmiō-Tennō, the Empress (43rd Emperor), 47, 51
Genkai Sea, 17
Gensan, 219
Genshō, the Empress (44th Emperor), 47, 48
Germany, 232
Go-Daigo-Tennō, 96th Emperor, 97, 98, 101, 102, 103, 104, 105, 106
Go-Fukakusa-Tennō, 89th Emperor, 96, 97
Go-Fushimi- Tennō, 93rd Emperor, 96
Go-Horikawa-Tennō, 73rd Emperor, 90
Go-Kameyama-Tennō, 99th Emperor, 106
Go - Kashiwahara - Tennō, 104th Emperor, 118, 120
Go-Komatsu-Tennō, 100th Emperor, 106
Go-Mitsunoo-Tennō, 108th Emperor, 149
Go-Murakami-Tennō, 97th Emperor, 105
Go-Nara-Tennō, 105th Emperor, 118, 120
Go-Reizei-Tennō, 67
Goriōkaku, fortress of, 198
Go-Saga-Tennō, 88th Emperor, 96
Go-Shirakawa-Tennō, 77th Emperor, 75, 77, 78, 80
Go-Sunjō-Tennō, 71st Emperor, 71
Go-Toba-Tennō, 82nd Emperor, 80, 85, 89, 90, 93
Go-Tsuchimikado-Tennō, 103rd Emperor, 118, 120
Go-Uda-Tennō, 91st Emperor, 92, 96
Gotō Yūjō, 117
Gregorian calendar, introduction of, 206

H

Hagi, 210
Hai-yang, island of, 224

INDEX

Hakata, bay of, 91
Hakodate, 180
Hakone, mountains of, 102
Hamada Yahei, 159
Ham-gyung, 138
Han (Kan), 17
Hang-tschou, 228
Hara, fortress of, 163
Harakiri, 152, 154, 197
Harris Kam, 180
Hasekura Tsunenaga, 158
Hataka, town of, 126
Hatakeyama family, the 110, 113, 119
Hayashi Daigaku-no-kami, 166
Hayashi Dōshun, 165
Hayasui, straits of, 9
Heguri, 27
Heiankiō, 51
Heijei-Tennō, 51st Emperor, 51, 52
Hekiteikan, 138
Hidachi, province of, 62, 63, 170
Hidetada, 145, 149
Hidetata, 162
Hidetsugu, 137
Hideyori, 146
Hieda-no-Ares, 48
Hiei, hill of, 102, 104
Hiei, temple of, 53
Higashiyama-Tennō, 113th Emperor, 170
Hikohohodemi-no-Mikoto, grandfather of the 1st Emperor, 8
Hiōgo (Kōbe), 103, 180, 199
Hirata Atsutane, 174
Hirato, island of, 126, 157
Hiroshima, 224
Hishikawa Moronobu, the painter, 167
Hiūga, province of, 8
Hōjō family, the, 87, 89, 98, 121, 140
Hōjō Sōun (or Ise Naganji), 121
Hōjō Takatoki, 97, 98
Hōjō Tokimasa, 77, 79, 88
Hōjō Tokimune, 91, 92, 96
Hōjō Tokiyuki, 102
Hōjō Yasutoki, 90
Hōjō Yoshitoki, 88, 89, 90
Hōki, province of, 98

Hōkotō, 228
Holland, 179, 182, 198
Hōnen-Shōnin, Buddhist priest, 94
Hou-na-kwanling, 241
Honnōji, fortress of, 132
Honto, island of, 7, 246
Hōōdō, royal temple of, 66
Horigoe, 115
Hōriūji, temple of, 31, 32
Hosokawa family, the 110
Hosokawa Katsumoto, 112
Hosokawa Masamoto, 118
Hosokawa Yoriyuki, 109
Hotta Masahiro, 180, 181
Hun-ho, the river, 243
Hupet, 228
Hwa-Yen (Ka-en-kō), 225

I

Iemitsu, 147, 148, 162
Ieharu, 172
Ienari, 172, 173
Iesada, 179
Ieshige, 172
Ietsugu, 170
Ieyasu, 169, 170
Ieyoshi, 178
Ii Naosuke, 181, 182
Iki, island of, 66
Ikoma, mountain of, 9
Imagawa family, the, 140
Imagawa Yoshimoto, 129
India, 31, 137, 157
Indian Ocean, 157
Inō-Chūkei, 177
Insignia of the Japanese Empire, 8
Iruka, 35
Ise, province of, 14
Ise Naganji (or Hōjō Sōun), 115
Ishida Mitsunari, 141, 142
Itagaki Taisuke, 208
Itakura Shigemasa, the general, 163
Itō Hirobumi, 215, 221, 228, 229
Itō Yukō, 224
Itō Jinsai, 166
Iwai, 25
Iwakura Tomomi, 208
Iwasa Matabei, the painter, 167
Izanagi-no-Mikotō, the god, 7
Izanami-no-Mikotō, the goddess, 7

INDEX

Izu, province of, 77, 79, 115, 121, 179
Izumo, province of, 7

J

Java, 157
Jesuits, the, 100, 161, 162, 171, 176
Jidō-Tennō, the Empress (41st Emperor), 48
Ji-miō-in, 97
Jimmu-Tennō, 1st Emperor, 8, 9, 10
Jingū-Kōgō, wife of the 14th Emperor, 16, 17, 18, 27
Jōchō, 66
Jōdō-Shū, Buddhist sect, 94
Jōei Year, 90
Joshin, the tribe, 66
Josten, Jan, 157
Jūnnin, 47th Emperor, 47
Juntoku-Tennō, 84th Emperor, 89, 93

K

Kada Azumamaro, 171, 174
Kagoshima, 126, 211, 212
Kai, province of, 13, 121, 170
Kaiping, fortress of, 225
Kakino-moto-no-Hitomaro, the song-writer, 50
Kamakura, 81, 85, 86, 97, 101, 102, 106, 110, 113, 114, 115, 118
Kameyana-Tennō, 90th Emperor, 96
Kamimura, Admiral, 240
Kami-worship, 26
Kammu, 50th Emperor, 51
Kamogawa, the river, 73
Kamo Mabuchi, 174
Kanagawa (Yokohama), 180
Kaneiji, temple of, 196
Kanō-Masanobu, the painter, 117
Kanō Tanniū, the painter, 167
Kantō, plain of, 13, 81, 101, 121, 135, 140, 170
Karak or Mimana, state of, 11, 16, 17, 24, 25
Kataoka, vice-admiral, 246

Katsushika Hokusai, the painter, 173
Katō Kiyomasa, 138, 139
Katsuragi, 27
Kawachi, province of, 21, 98
Kazusa, province of, 13, 121
Keichū, Buddhist priest, 166
Keikō-Tennō, 12th Emperor, 12, 13, 14
Keitai-Tennō, 26th Emperor, 3, 24
Keita, the Emperor, 27
Kemmu year, 101
Kenzo-Tennō, 23rd Emperor, 24
Khubitai-khan, 91, 92
Kiangsu, 228
Kiau-Tshou, port of, 232
Kibi-no-Makibi, the scholar, 49
Kibi-no-Tasa, 24
Kido Takayoshi, 188, 208
Kii, province of, 9, 170, 182
Ki-ja, Chinese prince, 16
Kimmei-Tennō, 29th Emperor, 25, 27
Kino Haseo, 60
Ki-no-Oyumi, general under the 21st Emperor, 24
Kin-Tshou, 241, 242
Kino Tsurayuki, 60, 65
Kiōtō, 51, 61, 62, 73, 85, 102, 103, 106, 109, 113, 116, 126, 130, 132, 135, 141, 147, 149, 161, 173, 175, 181, 184, 186, 199, 205
Kirino Toshiaki, major-general, 211
Kitamura Kigin, 166
Kitashirakawa-no-miya, prince, 229
Kin-lien-cheng (Kiū-ren-jō), fortress of, 225
Kiūsiū, island of, 8, 12, 18, 45, 103, 122, 125, 135, 138, 177
Kiyowara Takehira, the general, 73
Kizuki, village of, 7
Kobayakawa Takakage, 138
Koga Kubō, the, 114, 121
Kōfukuji, temple of, 73
Kōbun-Tennō, 39th Emperor, 43

INDEX

Koganei, Professor, 1
Kōgioku - Tennō, (Saimei - Tennō) 35th Emperor, 35, 41, 42
Kōgon-Tennō, 97, 98, 103
Ko-gu-ryu or Koma, 16, 17, 18, 24, 25, 41, 42
Kojiki, the, ancient Japanese Chronicle, 2, 3, 47, 174
Kōka, island of, 219
Kōkaku-Tennō, 119th Emperor, 172
Kōken the Empress, (46th Emperor), 47, 48, 49
Kōkō-Tennō, 58th Emperor, 58
Kōmiō-kōgō, wife of Shomu-Tennō 48
Kōmiō-Tennō, Emperor of the northern dynasty, 103
Ko-Mura Jutarō, 249
Kongōbuji, temple of, 53
Kōnin, 49th Emperor, 47, 51
Konishi Yoshinaga, 138
Kōno Moronao, 105
Konoe-Tennō, 76th Emperor, 74
Korea, 2, 11, 16, 18, 21, 24, 25, 41, 42, 45, 91, 124, 125, 137, 138, 139, 156, 169, 208, 218, 219, 220, 221, 222, 224, 225, 227, 228, 236, 237, 238, 240, 245, 246, 249, 250
Koreans, the, 2, 18, 21
Korpogurus, the, a race of dwarfs, 2
Kose Kanaoka, the painter, 60
Kōtoku-Tennō, 36th Emperor, 39, 41, 44
Kōza, temple of, 72
Kōzuke, province of, 97, 121
Kuang-Tscheng-Tse, 249
Kūkai, Buddhist priest, 53, 65
Kumano, temple of, 72
Kumamoto, town of, 210, 211, 212
Kuma-no-Ura, 9
Kumaso, race of, 12, 16
Kurile islands, 218
Kurino, Japanese Ambassador at St. Petersburg, 238
Kuropatkin, 240, 241, 243
Kusuko, wife of Heijei-Tennō, 52
Kusunoki Masashige, 97, 98, 103, 104, 105

Kusunoki Masatsura, 104, 105
Kwan-tshou, bay of, 233

L

Lian-tung peninsula, 225, 226, 228, 229, 232, 234
Liau-ho (Riōka), 227
Liau-yang, 240, 242, 243
Liegnitz, 91
Li-Hung-Tschang, 221, 228

M

Maeda Toshiie, 141
Ma-han (Bakan), 17
Makarov, admiral, 239, 240
Mamiya straits, 177
Manchuria, 66, 177, 225, 233, 234, 237, 240, 249
Manchurians, the, 2
Mangkan, King of the Mongols, 91
Marco Polo, the Venetian traveller, 92
Maruyama Okio, the painter, 173
Masatomo, 114, 115
Masuda Tokisada, 162, 163
Matsudaira Katamori, prince of Aizu, 186, 193, 194, 195, 196, 197
Matsudaira Nobutsuna, 163, 165
Matsudaira Sadanobu, 172, 173
Matsunaga family, the, 130
Matsunaga Hisahide, 119
Matsuo Bashō, the song-writer, 166
Mediterranean, the, 245
Mexico (Nova Hispania), 157
Michinoomi - no - Mikoto, general under the 1st Emperor, 9
Michizane, 59, 60
Midō, temple of, 65
Mikawa, province of, 140
Minamoto, the, 63, 67, 73, 77, 79, 81, 85, 86, 88, 89, 93, 140, 145
Minamoto Tsune-moto, 63
Minamoto Yoritomo, 79, 80, 81, 85, 86, 87, 88, 188
Minamoto Yoshinaka, 80, 81
Minamoto Yoshitomo, 74, 76, 77
Ming, Chinese dynasty of, 124, 159
Mino, province of, 130

Mishihase or Makkatsu, 41
Mito, 166, 182, 188
Miya, 169
Miyako, 198
Miyako-no-Yoshika, the scholar, 52
Miyoshi Chōkei, 119
Miyoshi family, the, 130
Miyoshi Kiyoyuki, the scholar, 60
Mizuno Tadakuni, 178
Mochiuji, 113, 114
Mommu, 42nd Emperor, 44, 47
Mongolia, 91, 124
Mongolian nations, languages of, 2
Mononobe family, the, 34
Mononobe-no-Arakahi, general under the Emperor Keitai, 25
Monotobu, the painter, 117
Mori family, the, 122, 130, 133
Mori Motonari, 122
Morinaga, prince, 101, 102
Moriya, son of Mononobe-no-Okoshi, 28
Motoori Norinaga, 174
Mototsune, 58, 59
Mukden, 243, 245
Murakami-Tennō, 62nd Emperor, 64
Murasaki-Shikibu, 65
Muro Kiūsō, 171
Musashi, province of, 121
Mutsu, chief town of the Ainus, 13
Mutsu, province of, 67, 73, 87, 122, 167
Mutsuhito, present Emperor of Japan, 188, 199
Mutsu Munemitsu, 228, 231

N

Nagasaki, 147, 164, 171, 176, 177, 178, 180, 205, 209, 219
Nagasunehiko, rebel in the reign of the 1st Emperor, 9
Nagato (Chōshū), 184
Nagato, prince of, 186, 187, 188, 198, 193, 194, 195, 202
Nagoya, port of, 138
Nakae Tōju, 166
Nakano-ōe-Oji, name of 38th Emperor before his accession, 35, 39, 41, 42

Nakatomi-no-Kamatari, originator of the fall of the Soga family, 35, 39, 42, 44, 57
Naniwa (Osaka), 9, 28, 45
Naniwa, palace at, 22
Naohito, prince, 170
Nara, 47, 49, 51, 93, 147
Narinaga, prince, 101
Nawa Nagatoshi, 97, 98
Nebugatov, rear-admiral, 248
Nichiren-Shōnin, Buddhist priest, 94
Nichiren-Shū, Buddhist sect, 94
Nigihayahi-no-Mikoto, relative of the 1st Emperor, 9
Nihonshoki, or Nihongi, ancient Japanese Chronicle, 2, 3, 16, 18, 21, 48
Niiagata, 180
Nikkō, 147
Ninigi-no-Mikoto, grandson of Amaterasu-Omikami, 8
Ninnaji-no-miya Yoshiaki, Prince, 195
Nintoku-Tennō, 16th Emperor, 22
Nitta family, the 97
Nitta Yoshishada, 97, 102, 103
Niu-tschwang, 227, 233
Nobuatsu, 165
Nobunaga, 130, 131, 132, 133, 134, 140
Nobuyori, 76
Nogi, general, 242
Norinaga, prince, 101
Noriyori, 88
Nozu, lieutenant-general, 224, 227, 242.

O

Oama, prince, 43
Oda family, the 123, 129, 130, 134
Oda Nobuhide, 129
Oda Nobunaga, 120, 123, 129, 161
Odawara, stronghold of the Hōjō family, 135
Ogata Kōrin, the painter, 167
Ogimachi-Tennō, 106th Emperor, 118, 130
Ogiū Sorai, 171
Oiwa, son of the general, Ki-no-Oyumi, 24

INDEX 257

Ojin-Tennō, 15th Emperor, 18, 21
Okehazama, battle of, 130
Oki, island of, 97, 98
Okinoshima, 247
Okitomo, 172
Oku, general, 242
Okubo Toshimichi, 188, 208
Okuma Shigenobu, 231
Okuninushi-no-Mikoto, 7
Omi, province of, 13, 131
Omi-no-Mifune, the scholar, 52.
O-Muraji, or Mononobe-no-Okoshi, 27, 28
Omura, 157
Onin years, 113, 120
Ono Harunaga, 145
Ono-no-Takamura, the scholar, 52
O-no-Yasumaro, 47, 48
Ono-no-Yoshifuru, 63
O-omi, or Soga-no-Iname, 27, 28
Osaka, port of, 135, 141, 146, 147, 167, 194, 195, 205
Osakabe, prince, 44
Oshikōchi Mitsune, the song-writer, 60
Osumi, province of, 12
Ota Dōkan, 117
Otomo, 157
Otomo family, the 122
Otomo-no-Kanamura, the chancellor, 24
Otori Keisuke, 196, 197
Ouchi family, the 122, 125
Ouchi Yoshioki, 119
Ouchi Yoshitaka, 122
Owari, or Atsuta, province of, 13, 14, 123, 129
Oyama Iwao, field-marshal, 225, 242, 243
Oyumi Kubō, the, 121

P

Pacific Ocean, 157, 158
Pak-je or Kudara, 16, 17, 18, 21, 23, 24, 25, 41, 42
Pak-je, King of, 27
Paul V. (Pope), 122
Peking, 91, 220, 233
Perry, admiral, 178, 179, 189
Pfhung-dō (Hōtō), island of, 223

Philip II. of Spain, 158
Philip III. (of Spain), 122
Phillippines, the, 137, 157
Phön han (Benkan), 17
Phyöng-Yang (Heijō), capital of Chōsun, 17, 138, 224
Pi-Asje wo, 241
Port Arthur (Rio-jun-Kō), 225, 229, 232, 233, 239, 241, 242, 243, 244, 245, 249
Portsmouth, Peace of, 249
Portugese, the, 126, 156
Postsan-han (Kan), 17
Prussia, 182
Pyön-chin, 17

R

Rai Sanyō, the historian, 175
Reizei-Tennō, 63rd Emperor, 64
Richardson, 185
Rihaku, Chinese writer, 49
Ri-Ki, King of Korea, 219
Rinoji-no-miya, Prince, 196
Riūkiū, island of, 205
Riūkiū, King of, 156
Riūzōji family, 122
Rokuhara-Tandai, 90
Rome, 158
Roosevelt, Mr., 248
Rosen, 249
Rovjestvensky, admiral, 245, 248
Russia, 91, 176, 179, 182, 228, 229, 232, 234, 236, 237, 238, 243, 244, 248, 249

S

Sadatoki, 96, 97
Saga district, the 209
Sagami, province of, 13, 85, 121, 178
Saga-Tennō, 52nd Emperor, 52
Saghalien, 177, 218, 246, 250
Saichō, Buddhist priest, 53
Saigiō, Buddhist priest and poet, 93, 94
Saigō Kirino, 212
Saigō Takamori, general, 188, 208, 209, 210, 211
Saitō family, the, 130
Sakai, 147

Saka-noae-no-Tamuramaro, the general, 51
Samurai, the, 86, 93, 105, 121, 148, 151, 153, 154, 170, 173, 182, 184, 201, 204, 205, 207, 208, 209, 210, 211
Sanetomo, 88
San-ho, plain of, 243, 244
Sanuki, province of, 75, 81
Sasebo, port of, 238
Sashiura, village of, 62
Sassa Norimasa, 135
Satsuma, prince of, 201
Satsuma, 126, 170, 185, 186, 187, 188, 194, 195, 202, 208
Schiroyama, 212
Schuschi, 228
Seimei-ō, King of Pak-je, 25
Seishōnagon, 66
Seisō, Emperor of China, 125
Seiwa-Tennō, 56th Emperor, 58
Sekigahara, plain of, 141
Sendai, town of, 122
Senjimon, the poem, 21
Seonghwan (Sei-kan), 223
Seoul, 138, 220, 222, 223, 224, 239
Sesshū, the painter, 117
Seto, inland sea of, 9, 62
Settsu, province of, 45
Seymour, Sir Edward, 234
Shanghai, 206
Shantung, 225, 226, 232
Shiba family, the 110, 113, 129
Shibata Katsuie, 134
Shiga, town of, 42
Shigemori, 79
Shigeuji, 114
Shijōnawate, field of, 105
Shikoku, island of, 75, 122, 170
Shimabara, peninsula of, 163
Shimatsu family, the 122
Shimatsu Saburō, 185
Shimatsu Yoshihisa, 135
Shimoda, 179, 180
Shimonoseki (Bakan), Peace of, 228, 236
Shimōsa, province of, 62, 63, 114, 121, 196
Shimozuke, province of, 49, 121, 196

Shinano, province of, 13, 80
Shingonshū, the, Buddhist sect, 53, 94
Shinikei, 138
Shinowara Kunimoto, 211, 212
Shinran-Shōnin, Buddhist priest, 94
Shinsai, 76
Shintoism, 27, 175
Shionoritsuhiko-no-Mikoto, leader of the army under Sujin-Tennō, 11
Shirakawa, 197
Shirakawa-Tennō, 72nd Emperor, 72, 73, 74
Shi-sen, battle of, 139
Shishi-ga-dani, village of, 78
Shitennōji, temple of, 31
Shizugadake, battle of, 134
Shōmu, 45th Emperor, 47, 48, 49
Shōtoku, son of the 33rd Emperor, 30, 31, 34, 35
Shōtoku, 48th Emperor, 47
Shugenshō, Chinese family, 124
Shugo, 110
Shunkan, the priest, 78
Siam, 158
Siberia, 176
Silesia, 91
Sil-la, or Shiraki, state of, 11, 16, 17, 24, 41, 42
Sil-la, king of, 25
Skikoku, island of, 135
Sōbin, 39
Soga family, the 27, 29, 34, 35, 36
Sŏng-hwan, 224
Soshōkun, 138
South America, 158
Sōya, straits of, 246
Spain, 158
Spaniards, the, 126, 156, 176
Stark, admiral, 239
Stössel, 240, 241, 243, 244
Sugawara family, the 59
Sugawara Michizane, 65
Sugawara, the scholar, 60
Suiko-Tennō (the Empress), 33rd Emperor, 3, 25, 30, 47
Suinin-Tennō, 11th Emperor, 14

INDEX

Sujin-Tennō, 10th Emperor, 11, 17
Sumpu, 147
Suō, province of, 126
Suruga, province of, 13, 158
Susa-noo-no-Mikoto, the god, 7
Sushūn, the Emperor, 30
Sutoku-Tenno, 75th Emperor, 74
Sutschou, 228
Su-Yung-Fu, 229
Suzaku-Tennō, 61st Emperor, 62
Szet-schnan, 228

T

Tabaruzaka, battle of, 211
Tachibanahime, princess, 13
Taidong, the river, 224
Taihō year, 44
Taika reforms, 39, 57, 87
Taira family, the, 63, 67, 73, 76, 77, 78, 79, 80, 81, 86, 89, 93, 129
Taira Kiyomori, 74, 76, 77, 78, 79, 80, 81
Taira Masakado, 62, 63
Taira Sadamori, 63
Tai-Wön-Kun, 219, 220
Takahira Kogorō, 249
Takakura-Tennō, 80th Emperor, 78, 79
Takamuko-no-Kuromaro, 39
Takamatsu, fortress of, 131, 133
Takamori, 212
Takano Chōei, 177
Takeda family, the, 131
Takeda Shingen, 121, 130
Takenoshima, 248
Takeuchi family, the, 27
Takeuchi-no-Sukune, minister of Jingu-Kōgō, 16
Takeuchi Skikibu, 175, 176
Takigawa Katsumasu, 134
Taku, fort of, 234
Takuma Tamenari, the painter, 66
Talien-wan (Dairen), port of, 233, 249
Tamagawa, the river, 167
Taneda, major-general, 210
Tanegashina, island of, 126
Tani Motoki, major-general, 211
Tankei, the carver, 95
Tanuma Okitsugu, 172
Teiseikō, 159

Temmu-Tennō, 40th Emperor, 48
Tendai, the, Buddhist sect, 53, 94
Tenji-Tennō, 38th Emperor, 42, 43, 44, 57
Tenshu, fortress of, 131
Terajima Munenori, 230
Tibetans, language of the, 2
Tien-tschwang-tai (Den-shō-dai), 227
Tientsin, 221, 222, 223, 224
Ting, admiral, 226
Toba-Tennō, 74th Emperor, 74
Todaiji, temple of, 49
Tōgō, 223
Tōgō Heihachiro, vice-admiral, 238, 239, 240
Tōgō Masaji, Rear-Admiral, 246, 247
Togukawa family, the 140, 149, 152, 182
Togukawa Iesato, 196
Tokugawa Ieyasu, 130, 134, 135, 140, 141, 142, 145, 146, 147, 148, 156, 157, 162, 165
Togukawa Yoshinobu, 182, 188, 194, 195, 196
Toho, Chinese writer, 49
Tokihira, 60
Tōkiō, 141, 145, 157, 201, 205, 206, 211, 224, 229, 250
Tokiyori, 90
Toku-ri-ji, 242
Toneri, prince, 48
Tō-no-mine, temple of, 43
"Torikaebaya-monogatari," the satire, 66
Tosa, 188, 193, 194, 195, 202
Tosa Mitsunaga, the painter, 95
Tosa Mitsuoki, the painter, 167
Tosa, prince of, 199
Toyotomi family, the, 141, 142, 145
Toyotomi Hideyoshi, the general, 131, 132, 133, 134, 135, 136, 137, 138, 139, 140, 141, 156, 162
Trans-Siberian railway, 232
Tschekiang, 228
Tschemulpo, 219, 220, 223, 239, 240

Tsching, Manchurian dynasty of, 159
Tschung-King, 228
Tshinampo, 240
Tsuboi, Professor, of Tokio, 2
Tsuchikumo, people of, 10
Tsugaru, straits of, 245
Tsukushi, province of, 17, 45, 67
Tsunayoshi, 165
Tsushima, island of, 66, 156
Tung-shan, island of, 233
Turks, language of the, 2

U

Uda-Tennō, 59th Emperor, 58, 59
Uesugi family, the 114
Uesugi Kagekatsu, 141, 142
Uesugi Kenshin, 121
Uesugi Noritada, 114
Uesugi Norizane, 113, 114
Ugayafukiaezu-no-Mikoto, father of the 1st Emperor, 8
Uji family, the, 33
Uji, town of, 65, 66
Uji-no-Wakairatsuko, son of the 15th Emperor, 21, 22
Ujitsuna, 121
Ujiyasu, 121
Ukida Hideie, 138
Ullong, island of, 247
Ulsan, mountain of, 139
Umako, chancellor of the Emperor Sushūn, 30, 34
Umako, son of Soga-no-Iname, 28
Unebi, mountain of, 10
United States, 178, 180, 181, 219, 248
Unkei, the carver, 95
Uraga, 178, 179
Uriu, rear-admiral, 238, 239

V

Vladivostock, 240, 245, 248

W

Wake-no-Kiyomaro, 49
Wani, 21
Watanabe Kazan, 177
Wei-hai-wei, fortress of, 226, 233
Witte, 249

X

Xavier, Francesco, 122, 126, 161

Y

Yalu, the river, 225, 227, 240, 241
Yamabe-no-Akahito, the song-writer, 50
Yamada, town of, 147
Yamada Nagamasa, 158, 159
Yamagata Aritomo, field-marshal, 224, 227
Yamagata Daini, 175
Yamaguchi (or Little Kiōtō) 122, 125, 126
Yamaguchi, lieutenant-general, 234
Yamaji, lieutenant-general, 225
Yamana Sōzen, the general, 112, 113
Yamana Ujikiyo family, the 109
Yamato, province of, 9, 21, 104
Yamatota-kern-no-Mikoto, son of the 12th Emperor, 12, 13, 14
Yamazaki, battle of, 133
Yang-tse-Kiang, 159
Yedo, 145, 147, 148, 156, 157, 167, 170, 173, 175, 176, 180, 184, 185, 195, 196, 201
Yellow Sea, the, 224, 238
Yen-Tschuan, 222
Yi-yu-Song (Rijiosho), 138
Yodo, the river, 167
Yokohama, 206
Yonekichi Miyake, Professor, 3
Yorii, 88
Yorimichi, 65
Yoshifusa, wife of Montoku-Tennō, 56th Emperor, 57
Yoshigumi, 119
Yoshimune, 170, 171, 172, 173
Yoshimasa, 113, 114, 116
Yoshimitsu, 106, 109, 110, 125
Yoshimochi, 110
Yoshino, village of, 104
Yoshiteru, 119
Yoshitsune, 77, 79, 81, 87
Yozei-Tennō, 57th Emperor, 58
Yūriaku-Tennō, 21st Emperor, 22, 24

For Product Safety Concerns and Information please contact our EU
representative GPSR@taylorandfrancis.com
Taylor & Francis Verlag GmbH, Kaufingerstraße 24, 80331 München, Germany

www.ingramcontent.com/pod-product-compliance
Lightning Source LLC
Chambersburg PA
CBHW060554230426

43670CB00011B/1814